American
Military Policy

POINT COUNTERPOINT

American Military Policy

Alan Allport

SERIES CONSULTING EDITOR
Alan Marzilli, M.A., J.D.

CHELSEA HOUSE
PUBLISHERS

A Haights Cross Communications Company

Philadelphia

CHELSEA HOUSE PUBLISHERS

VP, NEW PRODUCT DEVELOPMENT Sally Cheney
DIRECTOR OF PRODUCTION Kim Shinners
CREATIVE MANAGER Takeshi Takahashi
MANUFACTURING MANAGER Diann Grasse

Staff for AMERICAN MILITARY POLICY

EXECUTIVE EDITOR Lee Marcott
SENIOR EDITOR Tara Koellhoffer
PRODUCTION EDITOR Megan Emery
PHOTO EDITOR Sarah Bloom
SERIES AND COVER DESIGNER Keith Trego
LAYOUT 21st Century Publishing and Communications, Inc.

A Haights Cross Communications Company

http://www.chelseahouse.com

First Printing

1 3 5 7 9 8 6 4 2

Library of Congress Cataloging-in-Publication Data

Allport, Alan, 1970-
  American military policy / Alan Allport.
      p. cm. — (Point/counterpoint)
Includes index.
Summary: Presents arguments for and against America's role as global policeman, the
reduction of our nuclear arsenal, and the need for a ballistic missile defense shield.
  ISBN 0-7910-7488-9
  1. United States—Military policy—Juvenile literature. [1. United States—Military
policy.] I. Title. II. Series: Point-counterpoint (Philadelphia, Pa.)
  UA23.A5937 2003
  355'.033573—dc22

                                        2003013665

CONTENTS

Introduction
Alan Marzilli, M.A., J.D.
Durham, North Carolina

The debates presented in POINT/COUNTERPOINT are among the most interesting and controversial in contemporary American society, but studying them is more than an academic activity. They affect every citizen; they are the issues that today's leaders debate and tomorrow's will decide. The reader may one day play a central role in resolving them.

Why study both sides of the debate? It's possible that the reader will not yet have formed any opinion at all on the subject of this volume—but this is unlikely. It is more likely that the reader will already hold an opinion, probably a strong one, and very probably one formed without full exposure to the arguments of the other side. It is rare to hear an argument presented in a balanced way, and it is easy to form an opinion on too little information; these books will help to fill in the informational gaps that can never be avoided. More important, though, is the practical function of the series: Skillful argumentation requires a thorough knowledge of *both* sides—though there are seldom only two, and only by knowing what an opponent is likely to assert can one form an articulate response.

Perhaps more important is that listening to the other side sometimes helps one to see an opponent's arguments in a more human way. For example, Sister Helen Prejean, one of the nation's most visible opponents of capital punishment, has been deeply affected by her interactions with the families of murder victims. Seeing the families' grief and pain, she understands much better why people support the death penalty, and she is able to carry out her advocacy with a greater sensitivity to the needs and beliefs of those who do not agree with her. Her relativism, in turn, lends credibility to her work. Dismissing the other side of the argument as totally without merit can be too easy—it is far more useful to understand the nature of the controversy and the reasons *why* the issue defies resolution.

The most controversial issues of all are often those that center on a constitutional right. The Bill of Rights—the first ten amendments to the U.S. Constitution—spells out some of the most fundamental rights that distinguish the governmental system of the United States from those that allow fewer (or other) freedoms. But the sparsely worded document is open to interpretation, and clauses of only a few words are often at the heart of national debates. The Bill of Rights was meant to protect individual liberties; but the needs of some individuals clash with those of society as a whole, and when this happens someone has to decide where to draw the line. Thus the Constitution becomes a battleground between the rights of individuals to do as they please and the responsibility of the government to protect its citizens. The First Amendment's guarantee of "freedom of speech," for example, leads to a number of difficult questions. Some forms of expression, such as burning an American flag, lead to public outrage—but nevertheless are said to be protected by the First Amendment. Other types of expression that most people find objectionable, such as sexually explicit material involving children, are not protected because they are considered harmful. The question is not only where to draw the line, but how to do this without infringing on the personal liberties on which the United States was built.

The Bill of Rights raises many other questions about individual rights and the societal "good." Is a prayer before a high school football game an "establishment of religion" prohibited by the First Amendment? Does the Second Amendment's promise of "the right to bear arms" include concealed handguns? Is stopping and frisking someone standing on a corner known to be frequented by drug dealers a form of "unreasonable search and seizure" in violation of the Fourth Amendment? Although the nine-member U.S. Supreme Court has the ultimate authority in interpreting the Constitution, its answers do not always satisfy the public. When a group of nine people—sometimes by a five-to-four vote—makes a decision that affects the lives of hundreds of millions, public outcry can be expected. And the composition of the Court does change over time, so even a landmark decision is not guaranteed to stand forever. The limits of constitutional protection are always in flux.

These issues make headlines, divide courts, and decide elections. They are the questions most worthy of national debate, and this series aims to cover them as thoroughly as possible. Each volume sets out some of the key arguments surrounding a particular issue, even some views that most people consider extreme or radical—but presents a balanced perspective on the issue. Excerpts from the relevant laws and judicial opinions and references to central concepts, source material, and advocacy groups help the reader to explore the issues even further and to read "the letter of the law" just as the legislatures and the courts have established it.

It may seem that some debates—such as those over capital punishment and abortion, debates with a strong moral component—will never be resolved. But American history offers numerous examples of controversies that once seemed insurmountable but now are effectively settled, even if only on the surface. Abolitionists met with widespread resistance to their efforts to end slavery, and the controversy over that issue threatened to cleave the nation in two; but today public debate over the merits of slavery would be unthinkable, though racial inequalities still plague the nation. Similarly unthinkable at one time was suffrage for women and minorities, but this is now a matter of course. Distributing information about contraception once was a crime. Societies change, and attitudes change, and new questions of social justice are raised constantly while the old ones fade into irrelevancy.

Whatever the root of the controversy, the books in POINT/ COUNTERPOINT seek to explain to the reader the origins of the debate, the current state of the law, and the arguments on both sides. The goal of the series is to inform the reader about the issues facing not only American politicians, but all of the nation's citizens, and to encourage the reader to become more actively involved in resolving these debates, as a voter, a concerned citizen, a journalist, an activist, or an elected official. Democracy is based on education, and every voice counts—so every opinion must be an informed one.

This volume examines the role of the U.S. military in world affairs. That role has changed drastically since World War II, in which the United States took up arms only after the bombing of U.S. territory in Pearl Harbor. Starting with the postwar rebuilding of Europe and Asia, the United States has taken up the role of "global policeman," intervening in conflicts in Korea, Vietnam, the Middle East, and Eastern Europe. In spite of recent military victories in Afghanistan and Iraq during the ongoing "war on terror," many Americans have questioned whether the use of troops is morally justifiable when the nation is not under direct attack. The stated purpose of the Iraqi invasion was to search out and destroy "weapons of mass destruction," but the United States itself possesses an enormous stockpile of nuclear weapons built during years of tension with the former Soviet Union. Supporters of a strong U.S. military maintain that the nuclear arsenal is in responsible hands and serves as a deterrent to world conflict, with a ballistic missile defense system serving as backup. However, opponents of military buildup question whether nuclear weaponry and a "star wars" defense system are necessary in today's world. Emotions run high when military issues are debated: Many antiwar protesters believe that wars take innocent lives, but many Americans question the protesters' loyalty to their country. Regardless of position, everyone agrees that the consequences of the debate have profound effects throughout the world.

The Military Policy Debate

On Wednesday, April 9, 2003, U.S. tanks and armored vehicles rolled into the city center of Baghdad, the capital of Iraq, to the joyous cries of thousands of Iraqis celebrating the defeat of their leader, dictator Saddam Hussein. As statues of the detested Hussein were toppled all over Baghdad, watched by TV audiences across the world, the scale of America's military achievement in Iraq began to sink in. It was just 21 days since Operation Iraqi Freedom—the code name for the joint U.S.-British assault on Hussein's regime—had begun with a spectacular barrage of Tomahawk cruise missiles and bombs. In those three weeks, more than 300,000 coalition troops, including 255,000 U.S. servicemen and servicewomen, had seized control of much of southern and central Iraq, including the key port of Basra on the Persian Gulf. They had been supported by around 2,000 combat aircraft flying more than 30,000 separate missions, dropping 20,000 bombs and explosive devices, most of which were precision-guided (or "smart") munitions.[1]

> • **Do you think the United States has the right to invade another country, even if that country has not attacked Americans directly? What if that country had threatened to attack the United States?**

Perhaps most impressive of all was the low casualty rate sustained by the coalition force. As of April 9, only 130 American and British personnel had been killed, with a number of other troops wounded, captured, or missing. Compared to the D day invasion of Normandy, France, in June 1944, for example, when the United States suffered 3,000 casualties within just a few *hours* of the first landings—this was an extremely low figure. Meanwhile, Hussein's army, which before the start of Operation Iraqi Freedom was about 350,000 strong, had largely ceased to exist by the twenty-first day of the war. Whole divisions had melted away, partly because of coalition air and land attacks, but also because America's overwhelming military strike—known as the "Shock and Awe" campaign—had so terrified and bewildered Iraqi units that many simply had fled or surrendered without a fight. Even those critics who remained unconvinced that the war was just or wise admitted that the drive toward Baghdad had been rapid and highly impressive. One British expert on military science, who had been skeptical of earlier coalition strategy, said that the final Anglo-American push was "superbly choreographed."[2] Vice President Dick Cheney, who was closely involved in the planning of Operation Iraqi Freedom, was naturally even more effusive: The drive on Baghdad was, he said, "one of the most extraordinary military campaigns ever conducted."[3]

> • **Should the United States use its military power to encourage other nations to adhere to American values, such as democratic rule? What about using the military to topple corrupt or brutal dictators?**

The U.S.-led campaign against Saddam Hussein, and the strike on the Al Qaeda and Taliban terrorist networks in Afghanistan in 2001 (known as "Operation Enduring Freedom"), has created its own kind of "shock and awe" across the world: It has demonstrated once and for all that the United States now possesses a military superiority that is virtually unprecedented in human history. Barely a quarter of a century after its chastening defeat in Vietnam, the United States has reemerged as a superpower with a military strength that is second to none. Does this U.S. advantage represent a permanent change in the balance of global power, however, or

Extracts from the 2002 National Security Strategy of the United States of America.

The United States possesses unprecedented—and unequaled—strength and influence in the world. Sustained by faith in the principles of liberty and the value of a free society, this position comes with unparalleled responsibilities, obligations, and opportunity. The great strength of this nation must be used to promote a balance of power that favors freedom.

For most of the 20th century, the world was divided by a great struggle over ideas: destructive totalitarian visions versus freedom and equality.

That great struggle is over. The militant visions of class, nation, and race that promised utopia and delivered misery have been defeated and discredited. America is now threatened less by conquering states than by failing ones. We are menaced less by fleets and armies than by catastrophic technologies in the hands of the embittered few. We must defeat these threats to our nation, allies, and friends.

This is also a time of opportunity for America. We will work to translate this moment of influence into decades of peace, prosperity, and liberty. The U.S. national security strategy will be based on a distinctly American internationalism that reflects the union of our values and our national interests. The aim of this strategy is to help make the world not just safer but better. Our goals on the path to progress are clear: political and economic freedom, peaceful relations with other states, and respect for human dignity.

Source: Available online at http://www.whitehouse.gov/nsc/nss.html

DEFENSE CONTRACT MANAGEMENT AGENCY
Procurement, Defense-Wide
Fiscal Year (FY) 2003 Budget Estimates
($ in Millions)

Date: February-02

Appropriation: Procurement, Defense-Wide
P-1 Line Item Number: 21

Item	President's Budget		FY 2003 Budget Estimates					
	FY 2001		FY 2001		FY 2002		FY 2003	
	Quantity	Cost	Quantity	Cost	Quantity	Cost	Quantity	Cost
01 Passenger Carrying Vehicles	2	0.060	2	0.060	4	0.137	5	0.182
02 DCMA Functional Area Applications (FAA)	2	2.456	2	1.981	1	0.750	-	-
03 DCMA Communications & Computing Infrastructure (C&CI)	1	0.154	1	0.537	251	6.051	344	9.803
04 DCMA Related Technical Activities (RTAs)	1	1.064	1	0.843	-	-	-	-
05 DCMA Information Assurance (IA)	1	0.831	1	1.144	-	-	-	-
06 Standard Procurement System (SPS)	3	19.744	3	19.744	3	19.887	3	3.692
Total DCMA	10	24.309	10	24.309	259	26.825	352	13.677

Exhibit P-1C, Comparison Report

Maintaining its massive military is very expensive for the United States. This chart shows the expenditures for the fiscal years 2001 and 2002, compared with the president's military budget estimate for 2003. Note that all costs are listed in millions.

will it prove to be temporary and brittle? Is future American security through military strength guaranteed, or could arrogance—the sin of *hubris*, as the ancient Greeks called it—eventually topple the American giant?

The Costs of Superpower Status

Certainly, according to conventional calculations, America's military lead over the rest of the world is vast. Its regular armed forces of 1.5 million men and women include:

- 10 army and 3 marine divisions, with 11,000 heavy tanks and 30,000 other armored vehicles;

- 13 fighter wings, and more than 11,000 combat and support aircraft;

- a fleet of 239 warships, with carrier task forces able to project air and naval power across the globe; and

- a nuclear arsenal of 700 intercontinental ballistic missiles (ICBMs) and another 760 submarine and air-launched atomic weapons.[4]

- **Do you think the United States' enormous arsenal is a deterrent against possible aggressors? What kind of leaders or nations might not be intimidated by American military might?**

With such a battery of force, it is difficult to see how any would-be aggressor could hope to challenge the United States in a straightforward conflict. America's technological advantage—its dazzling array of hi-tech stealth fighters and bombers, "smart" bombs, and satellite-based communications and intelligence networks—is simply unmatched. Even the largest military forces that potentially oppose it, such as those of Russia or the People's Republic of China, are years, if not decades, behind in technical quality.

This mighty arsenal comes at a price, though, both literally and symbolically. As U.S. weapon systems have become more sophisticated, their costs have risen exponentially. For example, take the 4,400-pound (1,996-kilogram) GBU-28 "Bunker Buster," a smart bomb that was used to spectacular effect against Saddam Hussein's underground communications centers and headquarters in Iraq. Each Bunker Buster has a $145,000 price tag attached. When the costs of the aircraft and highly trained personnel required to use it are factored in, its expense rises even higher. As a result, the United States' wars create long invoices. It is estimated that during the first 25 days of Operation Enduring Freedom, the bombardment of Taliban positions cost approximately $300 million. In all, the Defense Department spent $1 billion a month in Afghanistan, while the liberation of Iraq is expected to eventually cost at least $80 billion—and probably more.[5] Running a war the American way is expensive. The United States already allots an annual $343.3 billion for its military, more than the next seven highest-spending world nations—Russia, Japan, France, the United Kingdom, Germany, China, and Italy—combined. As technology improves, the cost inevitably will grow larger. Every dollar invested in the U.S. armed forces means an extra dollar extracted from the American taxpayer or added to the already enormous U.S. national debt, and a dollar less available for other spending programs on health, education, and welfare. Can the economy of the United States take the strain of this ever-increasing burden?

- **Should the United States help police the world simply because it is the only nation that can?**

Power breeds commitments, too. As the old certainties of the Cold War era crumble, the United States has found itself drawn—willingly or not—into the role of "global policeman" in the new world order. The international situation today is very different from that of the Cold War, which lasted from the end

COST OF WAR ITEMS IN FY 03 BUDGET REQUEST		
ITEM	**RATIONALE**	**COST**
Operation Noble Eagle	Combat air patrols (CAPS) over U.S. cities	$517.3 million
Chemical/Biological Anti-terrorism Program	Initiative to boost homeland defense and protection of forces against increased post-Sept. 11 threat of terrorist chemical and biological attack	$480.1 million
Command, Control, Communications, Computers, and Intelligence (C4I)	Support Operation Enduring Freedom C4I requirements	$599.5 million
KC-135E tanker aircraft	Upgrade tanker engines to support Operation Enduring Freedom air refueling requirements	$89.0 million
Linguists	Hire linguists to support Operation Enduring Freedom translation requirements	$14.3 million
Tomahawk Land Attack Missiles	Convert remaining Tomahawk missiles to conventional version for use in war on terrorism	$598.0 million
Military Construction	Construct facilities to meet force protection and prisoner detainee requirements	$35.1 million
Munitions and Aircraft	Laser Guided Bombs, JDAMs, Global Hawk UAV, Predator UAVs, KC-130 used or lost in Operation Enduring Freedom	$422.6 million
War Pay	Personnel costs triggered by Operation Enduring Freedom related to hazardous duty incentive, imminent danger, family separation pays, and death gratuity	$320.8 million
TOTAL		**$3.1 billion**

NEW CONGRESSIONAL PROGRAMS		
ITEM	**RATIONALE**	**COST**
War Pay Enhancements	Included in manager's amendment to H.R. 4547 adopted on May 1, 2002	$182 million
Joint Task Force Support to Law Enforcement Agencies	Authorizes joint task forces to provide support to law enforcement agencies conducting counter-terrorism activities	$5 million
TOTAL		**$187 million**

It may be expensive for the United States to support such a powerful military, but many people argue that the security it provides is worth the cost. This table outlines the prices of certain military necessities and also provides reasons to support the expenditures.

of World War II in 1945 to the collapse of the Soviet Union in 1991. The Cold War was *bipolar,* meaning that the world was — with a few exceptions — divided into two opposing camps, led by the capitalist United States and the Communist Soviet Union. These rival superpowers vied for influence over smaller "satellite" powers in Africa, Asia, and the Middle East, and they amassed enormous nuclear stockpiles with which to threaten one another in a mutual "balance of terror." Life during the Cold War, with its constant ideological struggle between East and West and the ever-present risk of nuclear apocalypse, was often frightening. Paradoxically, however, there was also a lot of stability to it. Both sides were fairly evenly balanced, and so each was able to keep the other in check. The stalemate between the United States and the Soviet Union set the world in a kind of stasis; there was a reassuring predictability about the course of events. Despite fiery propaganda on both sides, neither superpower was ever really in a position to challenge the survival of the other.

This all changed when the Soviet Union and its allies in Eastern Europe collapsed at the end of the 1980s. The world became *multipolar*—there were suddenly many independent foci of power, and their behavior no longer could be predicted or controlled as easily as during the Cold War. In this new and unstable environment, the United States has found it increasingly necessary to intervene directly in the affairs of other countries when regional conflict or revolution threatens to escalate out of control. These peacekeeping responsibilities have sometimes been successful—as in Bosnia in 1995. At other times, though, such as in Somalia in 1993, they have ended disastrously, with American lives lost and the situation left no better than before. So-called "Rogue Nations"—countries that illegally possess nuclear, biological, or chemical "Weapons of Mass Destruction" (WMD) or that export terrorism abroad—have become a major perceived threat, inspiring acts of U.S.-led "regime change," such as the attack against Saddam

Hussein's Iraq. The fall of communism left America victorious in the Cold War, but the Soviet Union was replaced on the international stage by many new foes—smaller and weaker than the old Soviet Union, perhaps, but in some ways more difficult to deal with.

> • **Why might certain enemies, such as militant fundamentalists like Osama bin Laden, not be worried about reprisals from the United States after carrying out a terrorist attack?**

Perhaps most dangerous of all, the post–Cold War multipolar world contains a new type of enemy, one that is stateless and hidden. This is the international terrorist, led by religious fundamentalists such as Al Qaeda's Osama bin Laden. All the expensive weaponry in the U.S. military arsenal could not prevent a tiny cell of bin Laden's acolytes from committing acts of atrocious violence against American civilians on September 11, 2001. Even the lightning campaign against Al Qaeda's stronghold in Afghanistan was unable to fatally disrupt the organization or capture its commander. Bin Laden's supporters practice what is known as "asymmetric warfare." They attack the United States indirectly with isolated and surprise acts of terror rather than confront its vastly stronger armed forces face-to-face. This is not only a far more cost-effective method of fighting than conventional warfare, it is much harder to retaliate against. The U.S. air force can hardly flush out the covert Al Qaeda operatives who might be sheltered in American cities by bombing them. The uncomfortable reality facing American political leaders is that much of the expensive U.S. military stockpile is, in effect, useless in combating terrorism.

Strategic Options and Issues

This is not to say that the challenge of international terrorism is unanswerable, but it does suggest that, for all of America's very real strengths, the country will also face some difficult security decisions in the next few years, with no clear indication of which choices are the best ones. The road ahead is very uncertain.

There is, first of all, the question of whether America should commit itself wholeheartedly to the role of global policeman or whether it should restrict its activities purely to the defense of primary U.S. interests. Does the United States, as the world's only superpower, have a right, a responsibility, or even a moral obligation to concern itself with events in, say, the Middle East, Africa, and South America? One school of thought would say that global policing is inseparable from strategic primacy, whether Americans like it much or not. America's prosperity and defense depend upon the maintenance of peace throughout the world. The United States cannot ignore events in, for example, the disputed province of Kashmir in South Asia, because conflict between India and Pakistan (both of which claim the territory) would have disastrous consequences for the stability of the region, and ultimately for America's security. For the United States, upon which so many people and nations around the world depend for financial aid and other assistance, opting out of international affairs is simply not an available choice. Others would add that the United States ought to use its power aggressively to propagate Western values of democracy in despotic regions. Just as the nineteenth-century British Empire employed its maritime superiority to crush the African slave trade, so America should intervene to prevent mass violations of human rights and unseat tyrannical governments.

> • **When the United States deploys its military to places around the world, do you think it is helping other nations or interfering in their private affairs? Under what circumstances might a nation welcome American intervention?**

On the other hand, there is a strong counterargument that persistent American intervention around the world is neither wise nor just. The United States already has a host of commitments worldwide—its alliance with the Western European powers as part of the North Atlantic Treaty Organization (NATO), for example, and its defense of the western Pacific countries of Japan, South Korea, and Taiwan. Is it really in the nation's best interests to commit troops to interminable "quagmire" areas of conflict such as the Middle East or Central America when it already has responsibilities enough? Not only does this smack of old-style Western imperialism, but it also encourages "overstretch"—that is, taking on too

America Overstretched? Extracts from a 2002 Strategic Studies Institute Report on "Maintaining Strategic Balance."

The most important current mission for the Army is to make the maximum possible contribution to winning the war against terrorism. So far it has performed superbly as part of a joint force in varied operations in distant theaters. . . . Many commentators and administration spokesmen have described a new method of warfare involving Special Forces, airpower, and indigenous allies. This approach had great initial operational success in Afghanistan, and might be appropriate for the next stages of the war when applied in similar circumstances in the Philippines, Yemen, or Somalia.

However, operations against those nations described as an "axis of evil" by Bush will undoubtedly require much more extensive forces. The Army has already found it is running short of Special Forces soldiers just to meet current requirements. Wherever the next operations are conducted, they are certain to place a heavy load on the Army, if not for significant combat operations, then certainly for peace operations, assurance, and deterrence. Performing all these missions well will be essential for strategic victory, and they will not be easy or short in duration. Major General Richard Cody, commander of the 101st Airborne, has described his unit's mission in Afghanistan as a "marathon," a revealing term that describes projections of both the level of effort and time required. Strategic rationale may or may not exist for spreading the war . . . until adequate forces are available, though, the spread of the war on terrorism should be limited or at least carefully controlled.

Source: Available online at http://www.carlisle.army.mil/ssi/pubs/2002/hydra/hydra.htm

many military obligations at once—and it might cause a potentially fatal dispersion of American power away from homeland defense. It is also very expensive. To compound the problem, U.S. involvement in places such as Iraq, however well meaning, may be provoking exactly the kind of resentment against the "interfering" Americans that has incited sympathy in some parts of the Arab world for terrorists like bin Laden.

> • **How has the international climate changed since the Cold War ended? How do you think the American military should respond to those changes?**

Then there is the nuclear question. Cold War strategy was founded on the balance of power and terror between the United States and the Soviet Union—a tacit understanding on both sides that neither could provoke the other too far without triggering a nuclear attack that would devastate the world. Progress toward multilateral nuclear disarmament was painfully slow during the Cold War, but at least the mutual suspicion of both camps meant that nuclear weapons technology did not proliferate outside their control. The post-1991 environment is very different. The immediate risk of nuclear holocaust by an exchange of ICBMs between Russia and the United States has been vastly reduced. The splintering of the Soviet Union, however, has created new opportunities for atomic materials and know-how to fall into the hands of smaller nations—and perhaps even terrorist groups. In January 2002, North Korea, the last true despotic Communist country on Earth, announced that it was withdrawing from the international Nuclear Non-Proliferation Treaty, presumably in order to pursue the construction of weapons of mass destruction. The possibility of a second Korean War, fought this time with tactical atomic missiles, is a terrifying prospect.

Is it prudent, then, for the United States to maintain its high current level of nuclear weapons as an ultimate deterrent against

North Korea, often considered a rogue nation because of its aggression toward its neighbors and its unpredictability, withdrew from the Non-Proliferation Treaty in 2002. This caused many observers to fear that North Korea intended to build nuclear weapons, which would set the stage for a possible second Korean War. Seen here in a 1996 U.S. spy satellite photo are some of North Korea's spent nuclear fuel rods.

aggressors? Or does the existence of this arsenal only encourage the development of a new multipolar arms race, as well as open up the possibility of atomic missile launches and explosions by accident? Is the idea of a Ballistic Missile Defense (BMD) system—a network of interceptors to track and destroy incoming ICBMs before they can reach the United States or its allies—the antidote to the nightmare of nuclear attack? Or is such a system both technically unfeasible and likely to worsen rather than improve the international security situation?

As one recent writer on American national security problems after 1991 puts it:

> [T]he transition to a post–Cold War environment was expected to be simple and much cheaper. We now know that this is not the case; indeed, the period since the fall of the Soviet Union has been far more complicated in many ways, culminating with the tragic events in the United States on September 11, 2001.[6]

———————————●———————●———————●————————

As informed citizens, Americans must seek to understand these complications and the taxing military and security problems that they present for the new millennium.

The United States Must Accept the Role of Global Policeman

I n the fall of 1995, many Washington lawmakers and pundits leaped to the attack when President Bill Clinton announced his intention to commit American ground troops to peacekeeping activities in Bosnia-Herzegovina, the war-wracked province of former Yugoslavia that was seething with dangerous ethnic tensions. "[Clinton's] going to suck us in, step by step," charged Colorado Congressman Joel Hefley. Like many critics of the policy, Hefley believed Bosnia might become a second Vietnam — a hopeless military quagmire involving an ever-increasing number of American troops and casualties — and that there would be no easy way to withdraw from the region.[1] More than 180 first-term members of the House of Representatives took the unusual step of signing a petition to the president, urging him not to deploy troops to Bosnia. Some politicians believed that the commitment was an act of reckless bravado intended merely to back up

The United States undertook one of its first peacekeeping efforts in Bosnia and Herzegovina, located on the site of the former Yugoslavia. The mission was quite successful and many argued that it could be a model for further American interventions in world trouble spots.

the president's earlier unofficial offer of support to the Bosnians. "We should not put American lives on the line just to rescue an outdated presidential promise," said John Ashcroft, then a senator (who became the U.S. attorney general in 2001).[2] Grim reminders of other international crisis zones were pointed out: "I don't want to see another Beirut," warned Illinois Representative Glenn Poshard.[3] Even among the president's supporters, the mood was somber and uncertain.

- **How did the American experience in Vietnam change people's attitudes toward overseas military commitments? Do you think the failure in Vietnam should preclude future military action?**

In fact, Operation "Joint Endeavor," as the NATO peace-keeping mission in Bosnia was called, turned out to be nothing like Beirut or Vietnam. The first contingents of the 20,000 troops of the 1st Armored Division deployed to the Balkans in December 1995 encountered little opposition to their presence, and they were able to conduct their peacekeeping assignments— monitoring ceasefire lines; brokering deals between the rival Serb, Croat, and Muslim communities; and investigating allega-tions of war crimes—with relative tranquillity. Almost a decade later, less than a quarter of the original American contingent remained in Bosnia. Although a small U.S. presence may stay in the country for some time to help with postwar reconstruction, the prospects for that area of the Balkans look quite hopeful— or at least a great deal better than they did back in the mid-1990s. U.S. intervention played an important role in returning peace to a combat zone and ending the cycle of brutal atrocities that had tormented the civilian population. Not only was this a valuable exercise in American values in action, but it also was very much in the enlightened self-interest of the United States. Security at home rests ultimately upon stabilizing war-torn areas like the Balkans.

Joint Endeavor and its successor operations in Bosnia

MAJORITY OF AMERICANS OPPOSE U.S. TROOPS IN BOSNIA	
U.S. troops in Bosnia	
Approve	41%
Disapprove	54%
U.S. will accomplish goals in Bosnia with few casualties	
Confident	40%
Not confident	57%
U.S. will accomplish goals with few casualties	
Bosnia in 1995	40%
Compared with Haiti in 1994	67%
Compared with Somalia in 1993	64%
U.S. troops in Bosnia will be withdrawn in one year	
Confident	46%
Not confident	50%
U.S. effort to establish peace in Bosnia will succeed	
Confident	44%
Not confident	51%

Sampling error +/- 3%
Source: CNN/USA-Today/Gallup Poll. Interviews with 1,000 adult Americans conducted December 15–18, 1995

When President Bill Clinton sent American troops to Bosnia in 1995, the reaction of the public was mixed. A large part of the population did not support the military effort, and many people feared there would be excessive casualties. This chart illustrates the results of a poll that asked American citizens how they felt about the Bosnian action in December 1995.

showed that American "global policing" *can* work successfully, so long as it is organized carefully and there is a clear political and military plan—rather than the kind of muddled crisis management that too often took place during the Cold War. The United States must accept its position as the preeminent world power and use its authority to spread key American values of freedom and the rule of law by encouraging democracy's supporters and punishing its opponents. Americans should not be afraid of exercising military muscle in the cause of international peace and prosperity.

The United States Often Has Been Too Slow Intervening Abroad

All foreign policy strategists agree that the United States should act to defend its vital interests in the world. The problem is in defining "vital interests." What is vital, and whose interests are at stake? It is clear that repelling an unambiguous challenge to the United States, such as a direct military invasion of its territory, would qualify as a vital interest. What about an attack on a neighboring country, though, or on a country with which the United States has friendly relations? How about a civil war or a revolutionary insurrection in a foreign land in which U.S. citizens and property are potentially at risk? Are these interests "vital" enough to trigger an American response? What about preemptive action, which seeks to remove an enemy government *before* it can launch an attack on the United States (as in the war against Iraq in 2003)? What if the interests of powerful U.S. corporations are in peril, rather than those of ordinary people? Is the nation compelled to defend the rights of General Motors or Standard Oil in faraway countries? There is no clear-cut answer to any of these questions, and each generation of Americans has had to renegotiate the scope of what it believes are its vital interests.

Up to the beginning of the twentieth century, the United States maintained a strongly isolationist attitude toward the rest of the world, meaning that it generally avoided what politicians called "foreign entanglements," such as alliances and interventions in wars abroad. This began to change during the 1901–1909 presidency of Theodore Roosevelt. Roosevelt, who had taken part in the Spanish-American War of 1898, one of the United States' first military ventures into the realm of international conflict, believed strongly that America was a growing power that had a responsibility as well as a right to exercise its influence overseas. Although he was out of office by that point, Roosevelt's ambitions were realized on a grand scale in 1917, when the United States intervened decisively in the European conflict that later became known as World War I. This marked the United States' first truly major break from isolationism.

- **What factors might have led the United States to expand its definition of its vital interests around the turn of the twentieth century? Do you think President Theodore Roosevelt was right in his belief that being a strong nation required the United States to exert its influence on the world stage?**

The 1905 Roosevelt Corollary to the Monroe Doctrine.

It is not true that the United States feels any land hunger or entertains any projects as regards the other nations of the Western Hemisphere save such as are for their welfare. All that this country desires is to see the neighboring countries stable, orderly, and prosperous. . . . [However,] chronic wrongdoing, or an impotence which results in a general loosening of the ties of civilized society, may in America, as elsewhere, ultimately require intervention by some civilized nation, and in the Western Hemisphere the adherence of the United States to the Monroe Doctrine may force the United States, however reluctantly, in flagrant cases of such wrong-doing or impotence, to the exercise of an international police power. . . . We would interfere with them only in the last resort, and then only if it became evident that their inability or unwillingness to do justice at home and abroad had violated the rights of the United States or had invited foreign aggression to the detriment of the entire body of American nations. . . .

There are, however, cases in which, while our own interests are not greatly involved, strong appeal is made to our sympathies . . . there are occasional crimes committed on so vast a scale and of such peculiar horror as to make us doubt whether it is not our manifest duty to endeavor at least to show our disapproval of the deed and our sympathy with those who have suffered by it. The cases must be extreme in which such a course is justifiable. There must be no effort made to remove the mote from our brother's eye if we refuse to remove the beam from our own. But in extreme cases action may be justifiable and proper.

However, even though World War I ended with the United States as the world's strongest nation, the country was still reluctant to continue an active foreign policy. This had dangerous implications when the Fascist regimes of Nazi Germany and militaristic Japan appeared on the world stage in the 1930s. Despite the danger that these countries represented to global peace and security, most American citizens opposed taking any firm action against them. The result was that the Nazis came very close to overrunning all of Europe by the end of 1941; and, on the other side of the world, the United States suffered a grievous military defeat when the Japanese attacked the U.S. Pacific Fleet at the Hawaiian naval base at Pearl Harbor. By refusing to join the Western democracies against German dictator Adolf Hitler as he expanded his power, and by turning a blind eye to Japan's aggression against China in the 1930s—or, in other words, by defining its vital interests too narrowly, and failing to take preemptive action— the United States imperiled its own survival. That same mistake must never be made again. As former Defense Secretary William Cohen said in his 1997 defense review, "If the United States were to withdraw from its international commitments, relinquish its diplomatic leadership, or relinquish its military superiority, the world would become an even more dangerous place, and the threats to the United States, our allies, friends, and interests would be even more severe."[4]

American Policing Guarantees World Stability

It may seem strange to say so at a time of terrorist threats and fears of war in the Middle East, but the world at the beginning of the twenty-first century is in many ways a very peaceful and stable place—certainly compared to the way it was 60, or even just 20, years ago. There is no imminent risk of a nuclear exchange between the superpowers of East and West, as there was throughout the Cold War. Europe, which was on the brink of total collapse and starvation at the end of World War II in

1945, is a prosperous and democratic continent. It is generally safe to travel and to transport goods and services across international borders. Communist autocracy has ended across much of the globe. According to an annual "Freedom in the World" report by the nonprofit organization Freedom House, for every country that became less free and democratic in 2002, three others became more so.[5] Of course, there are still many regions

Pro-Action in the National Interest.

Sometimes geopoliticians act as though determining the national interest were an arcane science, or at least an occult art. But there is nothing mysterious about the national interest. It is simply the set of interests that are widely shared by Americans in their relations with the rest of the world ... the national interest is broader than protection against geopolitical threats. The strategic interest is part of, but not necessarily identical to, the national interest. In a democracy the national interest is what a majority, after discussion and debate, decides are its legitimate long-run shared interests in relation to the outside world....

Why should Americans care about order in distant parts of the globe? The simple answer is that even distant disorder can have effects that hurt, influence, or disturb the majority of people living within the United States. The various ways in which these effects are transmitted are lumped together under the abstraction "rising interdependence." They add up to a world in which it is ever more difficult for us to isolate what happens inside the United States from what happens outside....

[T]here are two simple reasons why Americans have a national interest in reducing disorder beyond our borders. Things out there can hurt us, and therefore we will want to influence distant governments on a variety of issues, such as proliferation, terrorism, drugs, resources, and ecological damage. To do so, we will need power beyond just our good example. But there is sometimes another reason for concern about distant disorder: some foreign violations of human rights are so egregious that they evoke a broad response among Americans....

Source: Joseph S. Nye, Jr., "Why the Gulf War Served the National Interest," *The Atlantic Online*, http://www.theatlantic.com/issues/91jul/nye.htm.

suffering great hardships and injustices, such as sub-Saharan Africa and parts of Asia. Their plights remain as desperate as ever. Compared to the carnage and pessimism of the first half of the twentieth century, however, the world today is—in many important respects—doing quite well.

> • **How dependent do you think the world is upon the United States' leadership? Do you think the international community would become unstable if the United States were no longer the intimidating force it is now?**

There are many reasons for this, naturally, but one important factor is America's perceived willingness to prevent destabilization. So long as the United States is seen as a global policeman by the rest of the world, prepared to take action in the common interest if necessary, then confidence is maintained and would-be aggressors are deterred. As strategist and historian Donald Kagan has written: "The current, unusually stable condition of the world rests heavily on the belief in America's military power and commitment. If these are seen to decline, the stability and security of the world will decline apace." [6] The continuation of the world's stability cannot be taken for granted. It also cannot be denied that the United States' behavior has an enormous effect upon international stability. Should the United States decide to disengage from world affairs, defining its vital interests very narrowly and avoiding future "foreign entanglements," there is no other power to replace it. The result will be a more dangerous international order—one that the United States will ultimately have to address.

America Must Defend the Values to Which It Aspires

The United States aspires to authoritative moral goals: peace, democracy, and the pursuit of individual freedom and happiness. As President George W. Bush said to the graduating class of cadets at the U.S. Military Academy at West Point in June 2002: "America has no empire to extend or utopia to establish. We wish for others only what we wish for ourselves—safety from violence, the rewards of liberty, and the hope for a better life."[7] Such weighty objectives make it incumbent upon the United States to intervene across the globe when major infringements on human rights take place. To turn away on the grounds of cost or because "vital interests" are not affected is a failure to live up to those founding aspirations.

> • **Is the systematic killing of particular ethnic groups a legitimate reason for the United States to take military action? What about the desire to overthrow an oppressive regime, like that of former Iraqi leader Saddam Hussein?**

Perhaps the cruelest recent failure of that kind occurred in the African state of Rwanda in 1994. In one hundred days of terror, an estimated 800,000 people were murdered in a savage cycle of ethnic genocide. The United States and other Western powers did nothing to prevent the catastrophe from unfolding, even though there is strong evidence that they knew about the danger and could have acted swiftly.[8] Rwanda is an example of a case in which the United States rejected its global policing role, to its ultimate shame. Since the end of World War II and the revelation of the horrors of the Nazi Holocaust against Jews and other ethnic groups, the world has taken up the cry of "Never Again." Tragically, as Rwanda shows, that cry has not always been heeded. In other situations, though, such as Kosovo in 1999— where Albanian civilians were being expelled from their homes, and in many cases, mistreated and killed by Serbian militias— the United States responded with appropriate force. It is America's duty to follow the Kosovan, and not the Rwandan, precedent, to intervene decisively against tyranny and violence, however far-flung or supposedly "nonvital" the circumstances.

Sovereignty Should Not Be a Shield for Injustice

Some critics who oppose the intervention of the United States in other countries invoke the concept of state sovereignty. This is

The United States and the rest of the international community were slow to respond to the situation in Rwanda. By the time military intervention took place, hundreds of thousands of people had died in a systematic program of genocide in the African nation. Seen here are hundreds of human skulls that were placed on display during a genocide memorial held in Rwanda in April 1999.

the long-standing international law that guarantees the absolute right of members of the United Nations (UN) to conduct their own domestic affairs free from foreign interference. Why, they ask, should the United States be allowed simply to override the sovereignty of other nations when it so jealously guards its own? By what authority can it implement "regime change" against governments that it does not happen to like but which have not committed any overtly hostile acts against America? If one nation chooses to buck the law, what is to stop others from following the same dangerous precedent? Isn't that a recipe for global anarchy? It is true that state sovereignty, by outlawing meddling in other countries' affairs, has done much to prevent conflict and the exploitation of poor and weak nations by their wealthy and strong neighbors. This is an achievement that should not be taken lightly.

> • **How independent does the concept of sovereignty allow any given nation to be? If a country's leaders treat their people poorly, does sovereignty prevent other countries from stepping in to help the people?**

Sovereignty, however, was never intended to allow dictatorial governments to terrorize their populations, or, in effect, to make war on their own citizens. As a United Nations report on the problem points out:

> In a dangerous world marked by overwhelming inequalities of power and resources, sovereignty is for many states their best—and sometimes seemingly their only—line of defense ... [but] the defense of state sovereignty, by even its strongest supporters, does not include any claim of the unlimited power of a state to do what it wants to its own people.[9]

Nor was sovereignty conceived as a cloak to mask the secret support of terrorists by rogue nations. Although a just global policeman like the United States should not blithely disregard the rights of other countries to their autonomy under most circumstances, there comes a point where a government's callous disregard for the well-being of its citizens—such as in

Kosovo in 1999—or its funding and arming of terrorists—like Afghanistan's Taliban in 2001—overrides sovereign rights. No nation can hide behind its legal status in order to plan atrocities at home or abroad.

Journalist Michael Ignatieff has written, "Multilateral solutions to the world's problems are all very well, but they have no teeth unless America bares its fangs."[10] Global policing has risks and costs, but, as Ignatieff points out, the United States has an irreplaceable role. No other country can fulfill the kind

Possible Justifications for Going to War

- Invasion of the United States, as occurred at Pearl Harbor during World War II
- Invasion of a U.S. ally
- Threat of war against the United States
- Harboring terrorists who are threatening to the United States, as was the case in Afghanistan in 2001–2002
- Threat to Americans abroad
- Threat to U.S. economic interests
- Invasion of an "innocent" or "helpless" nation, as in Iraq's invasion of the defenseless Kuwait in the Persian Gulf in 1990–1991
- Civil war, as in the Balkans
- Genocide, as in Rwanda
- Tyranny

of responsibilities Americans can, or turn words into practical deeds. By embracing a sensibly broad understanding of national interest and being willing to act in defense of the global community, Americans will buttress international stability, honor their country's values abroad, and promote U.S. affluence and safety.

Policing the World Is Beyond Our Means and Not in Our Interests

E arly on the morning of October 23, 1983, a Mercedes truck was seen driving toward the International Airport complex in Beirut, Lebanon. Beirut in 1983 was the scene of a terrible and growing civil war between rival warlord factions that had seized power as the conflict between the Israeli Army and the Palestine Liberation Organization (PLO) in neighboring Israel spilled over into Lebanon, bringing chaos in its wake. To try to restore some order to the city, a multinational force of peacekeepers, including a large contingent of U.S. marines, had been deployed there. One unit of this force, the 1st Battalion, 8th Marines landing team, had set up its headquarters in a building compound at the city's airport. As the truck approached a security roadblock, it suddenly swung around without stopping and drove into the airport parking lot, circled around twice, then accelerated straight toward the marine headquarters. The horrorstruck

When Americans were killed in a terrorist bombing at the U.S. Embassy in Beirut, Lebanon, in 1983, many citizens expressed their fears that overseas military commitments would embroil the United States in another situation like the failed Vietnam War.

guards around the compound could do little in the few seconds that followed: They had been specifically forbidden to have their weapons loaded while they were on duty. The van crashed into the building's first floor, and a catastrophic detonation followed as more than a ton of explosives concealed in the truck went off. In all, 241 American marines, sailors, and soldiers died in the building collapse that followed, and 100 more were wounded. It was one of the worst days in the history of the U.S. military in peacetime.

> • **How was the tragedy in Beirut similar to the military failure in Vietnam? Did the two actions ultimately have the same effect on American military policy?**

Four months later, the U.S. marines completed their evacuation from Beirut. They had suffered grievous casualties yet had been unable to prevent the spread of a Lebanese civil war, which continued for years afterward. The marines themselves were not to blame for this sad failure. The mistake had been to rush them into a deadly situation with mysterious local politics that they did not really appreciate in order to do a peacekeeping job that they were not adequately trained or equipped to accomplish. One historical analyst of the Beirut tragedy put it this way: "The Marines . . . operated in a confusing environment under numerous restraints while executing a mission, which even today is not a primary mission nor fully understood."[1] By ordering its troops to serve as global policemen in 1983, the United States invited disaster.

The American experience in the Somalian capital of Mogadishu in October 1993 was a grim repeat of this experience. U.S. Rangers, acting as part of an international peacekeeping force trying to apprehend a local warlord, found themselves in a confused and deadly firefight with Somali militia. Eighteen American servicemen were killed in the melee, and the United States withdrew its forces shortly afterward. The well-meaning but ill-fated intervention solved nothing, and Somalia remains to this day a war-torn country in chaos.[2]

> • **How did the unsuccessful actions in Beirut and Somalia differ from more positive American military interventions like those in Afghanistan and Iraq? How well do you think the likelihood of success in a particular military encounter can be determined in advance?**

Since 1993 there have, of course, been more successful American interventions in other countries, such as the 1995 deployment to Bosnia, and more recently, the operations to liberate Afghanistan and Iraq from their tyrannical governments. The examples of Beirut and Mogadishu, however, serve as reminders that potential disaster lurks behind every attempt to reshape the world in the American image. The new era of forceful U.S. involvement in other parts of the globe that seems to have been inaugurated by Operations Enduring Freedom and Iraqi Freedom is fraught with risk, and it may bequeath tomorrow's America with unexpected responsibilities and burdens that are far removed from its vital interests. The United States would be well advised to avoid global policing.

Intervention Abroad Creates Burdens We Cannot Afford

There are always going to be occasions when it is right and necessary for the United States to take military action overseas. Even in the first years of the Republic, President Thomas Jefferson dispatched U.S. sailors and marines to punish the pirates of the "Barbary Coast" in North Africa, who had been waylaying and plundering American merchant vessels. This was an early and successful example of the United States' projecting power across the Atlantic Ocean. Today, with the threat of terrorist attack against the United States, it would be very shortsighted to abandon *any* possibility of intervention abroad. The problem with becoming the world's policeman and taking on too many responsibilities at one time, though, is that the nation may become hopelessly bogged down in overseas commitments. American armed forces are extremely powerful, but their resources are not inexhaustible.

- **Is the United States' status as the only superpower worth the expense required to maintain it? Which overseas commitments do you think are more important than others?**

Indeed, some military commentators are already warning that U.S. armed forces are dangerously overstretched. In a March 2003 report called "G.I. Woe", *Washington Monthly* editor Nicholas Confessore pointed out that, since the late 1990s, the U.S. army has been ordered to take on a new major deployment abroad on average every six months, and that pace is quickening. "During the first three months of 2003," Confessore continued, "the United States had more than twice as many troops on overseas missions at any given time as it did in 2000. It's getting harder to recruit new soldiers, and, on the whole, harder to keep the ones we have. . . . [T]hat can only mean decreased readiness,

"Global Leadership" — or World Policeman?

There is nothing wrong with "leadership" per se. The United States can and should play a leading role in a number of arenas. . . . Today's proponents of "global leadership," however, are advocating something better described as hegemony than as leadership. Unlike moral or economic leadership, global leadership does not envision the United States' leading by example or through diplomacy. Global leadership is essentially coercive, relying on "diplomacy" backed by threats or military action. . . .

The nebulous benefits of U.S. global leadership do not justify its immense costs, and it is unlikely that the United States is even capable of pursuing such a strategy over the long term. . . . And while trying to lead the world is costly enough now, a strategy that holds as its highest objective the exercise and preservation of American leadership seems likely to lead inexorably to an increase in commitments and costs over the long term.

Instead of trying to lead the world, the United States should concentrate on the protection of its vital national security interests. It can do so better by behaving as the "first among equals" in the community of great powers than by insisting that the United States, as the world's only superpower, can and should take responsibility for events all over the globe. Great power status does, after all, confer not only the ability to get involved in conflicts around the world but also the power to remain aloof from lesser quarrels.

Source: Barbara Conry, "U.S. 'Global Leadership': A Euphemism for World Policeman," *Cato Institute*, http://www.cato.org/pubs/pas/pa-267.html.

Costs of U.S. International Peace and Security Commitments Fiscal Year (FY) 1991–FY2001
(Budget authority in millions of current year dollars)

Operation	FY1991	FY1992	FY1993	FY1994	FY1995	FY1996	FY1997	FY1998	FY1999	FY2000	FY2001 to 06/30/01	TOTALS
AREAS OF ONGOING OPERATIONS												
Southwest Asia/Iraq												
Provide Comfort/Northern Watch	325.0	101.5	116.6	91.8	138.2	88.9	93.1	136.0	156.4	143.7	11.3	1,502.5
Southern Watch/Air Expeditionary Force	--	--	715.9	333.0	468.4	576.3	597.3	1,497.2	954.8	755.4	673.5	6,571.8
Vigilant Warrior	--	--	--	--	257.7	--	--	--	--	--	--	257.7
Desert Strike/Intrinsic Action/Desert Spring	--	--	--	--	--	--	102.7	5.6	13.8	239.8	207.2	569.1
Desert Thunder (Force Buildup, 11/98)	--	--	--	--	--	--	--	--	43.5	--	--	43.5
Desert Fox (Air Strikes, 12/98)	--	--	--	--	--	--	--	--	92.9	--	--	92.9
UNIKOM (UN/Iraq Observer Group)	21.5	4.9	6.0	--	--	--	--	--	--	--	--	32.4
Total Southwest Asia/Iraq	346.5	106.4	838.5	424.8	864.3	665.2	793.1	1,638.8	1,261.4	1,138.9	992.0	9,069.9
Former Yugoslavia (Bosnia)												
IFOR/SFOR/Joint Force	--	--	--	--	--	2,231.7	2,087.5	1,792.8	1,431.2	1,381.8	919.9	9,844.9
Other Former Yugoslavia Operations	--	5.8	138.8	292.0	347.4	288.3	195.0	169.9	155.4	101.3	61.5	1,755.4
Total Bosnia	--	5.8	138.8	292.0	347.4	2,520.0	2,282.5	1,962.7	1,586.6	1,483.1	981.4	11,600.3
Former Yugoslavia (Kosovo)												
Balkan Calm (Observer Mission, Pre-Air War)	--	--	--	--	--	--	--	--	34.6	--	--	34.6
Eagle Eye (Air Verification 10/98–03/99)	--	--	--	--	--	--	--	--	20.3	--	--	20.3
Noble Anvil (Air War)	--	--	--	--	--	--	--	--	1,891.4	--	--	1,891.4
Joint Guardian (KFOR)	--	--	--	--	--	--	--	--	1,044.5	1,803.1	931.4	3,779.0
Sustain Hope (Refugee Assistance)	--	--	--	--	--	--	--	--	141.6	--	--	141.6
Total Kosovo	--	--	--	--	--	--	--	--	3,132.4	1,803.1	931.4	5,866.9
Korea Readiness	--	--	--	69.7	90.9	--	--	--	--	--	--	160.6

Source: Under Secretary of Defense (Comptroller); FY2001 figures provided August 23, 2001.

Some opponents of U.S. military operations overseas worry that too many commitments will overstretch the nation's resources. In fact, the United States does spend astronomical amounts of money and labor on its peace and security actions abroad. This table contains information from the Department of Defense that outlines how much money was spent in 1991 through the first half of 2001 for specific overseas enterprises.

shrinking re-enlistments, lower morale, and, quite possibly, more mistakes."[3] The successful operations in Afghanistan and Iraq in 2001 and 2003 may have eliminated enemies of the United States and weakened the effectiveness of terror organizations such as Al Qaeda, but they have also left behind a legacy of peacekeeping that may continue for decades. By late spring 2003, the United States had about 255,000 troops either in Iraq or in the surrounding region. Many of these forces will be redeployed back to the United States or to other overseas bases once the mopping-up operations against Saddam Hussein's remaining forces are over. Some of them will have to remain, however, in order to prevent the fragile country from imploding into chaos. Estimates for the necessary post-liberation garrison range from 10,000 to 200,000. The point is that no one really knows what the nation's long-term commitment will need to be. If we embark on too many expeditions abroad, this continual drain on the country's security resources may begin to have a dangerous effect on the United States' ability to defend itself at home.

Global Intervention Damages U.S. Standing in the World

Is this encumbrance balanced out by the increased respect and authority America gains for its troubles? It would be comforting to think so, but the recent record suggests that global policing only undermines the United States' existing relationships with allies and international organizations. Furthermore, it creates resentment of American power that may have hazardous repercussions in the future. Far from buttressing its status by intervention abroad, the United States is actually alienating its supporters and creating new enemies.

> • **Why do you think people living in other countries often oppose U.S. involvement in their affairs? Do you think people's attitudes might be different if they are being led by an oppressive government? Why might that not be the case?**

It is important to remember that other countries often perceive U.S. policies very differently from the way Americans do. Where we might consider intervention in trouble spots necessary on security or humanitarian grounds, the same actions can be viewed as "interference" by people abroad. This is not simply because they "hate America," as some crude arguments have suggested. The attitude of the rest of the world toward the United States is much more complex than that. At the deepest level, America is a focus of widespread admiration. Its culture and values are attractive; millions of people abroad aspire to the American way of life. The problem as many of them see it is not that the United States is an inherently bad place, but that, as its power has grown, it has become increasingly arrogant. "What worries people around the world above all else," according to influential foreign policy analyst Fareed Zakaria, "is living in a world shaped and dominated by one country—the United States. And they have come to be deeply suspicious and fearful of us."[4]

This plays out in many different ways. In Europe, old and important allies such as France and Germany have distanced themselves from the United States. In the United Nations, America has been accused of acting in a heavy-handed and conceited way toward other, smaller member-states. In the Middle East, ordinary people—the so-called "Arab Street"—have reacted to U.S. interventions in Afghanistan and Iraq with anger, even though many of them had little love for the Taliban or Saddam Hussein. The problem with global policing is as much about appearance as reality. Even though the United States might have the best of intentions when it uses its military muscle abroad, foreign eyes can view the situation in a totally different way. Estranging a large proportion of the world's population will ultimately be very dangerous, even for as powerful a nation as the United States.

- **What changes in the world have caused former U.S. allies to oppose American military actions in recent years? Do you think the United States should be willing to act alone, even if its allies do not support it?**

Values Cannot Be Exported by Force

Can the United States actually rearrange the world according to its own model? Recently, there has been much talk of the concept of "nation building"—the process by which a foreign power such as the United States actively intervenes in a war-torn or chaotic country with large-scale aid and investment with the idea of creating a stable, prosperous, democratic, and friendly society. The belief is that if America re-creates trouble spots according to a certain template, then they will cease to be dangerous places and will help ease the United States' overall security problems. Quite apart from the cost and time required for nation building, however, there may be a more fundamental problem. "We tend to overlook a basic rule," says Boston University historian David Fromkin, "that people prefer bad rule by their own kind to good rule by somebody else."[5] No matter how generous it might seem, nation building looks like a form of old-style Western imperialism, which makes it more likely to be resented that greeted by its recipients.

> • **Do you think nation building is a good idea? What factors might make it possible for certain nations to be rebuilt on the American democratic model but not others?**

Advocates of nation building argue that there are successful test cases of such projects, such as the reconstruction of Germany and Japan after World War II. Are these examples relevant to places like Afghanistan, though? Gary Dempsey argues that the starting conditions are so different that the comparison is meaningless:

> The high level of education and industrial know-how in post-war Germany and Japan helped launch an economic recovery in both countries that is inconceivable almost anywhere else . . . the rule of law, property rights, free markets, and an entrepreneurial culture are what are necessary for economic success. Afghanistan has none of these things.[6]

It is simply implausible to presume that we can create mini-Americas around the world, and we should not be trying.

International Stability Is Undermined by Global Policing

Finally, what of state sovereignty? It is true that many dictators, such as Iraq's former leader Saddam Hussein, have exploited this important diplomatic concept to mask atrocities committed against their own people. There do need to be some internationally recognized safeguards to prevent this abuse, perhaps conducted under the auspices of the United Nations. The problem with arbitrarily picking and choosing moments to violate other nations' state sovereignty, as the United States has tended to do in recent years, is that it creates a dangerous precedent for other powers. This was illustrated in the immediate aftermath of Operation Iraqi Freedom, when India's government announced that it, too, reserved the right to conduct a preemptive strike against its longtime rival, Pakistan. The logic of India's argument was difficult for the United States to condemn without appearing hypocritical or inconsistent. As *The New York Times* put it, "If America can strike out at a suspected sponsor of terrorism and hugely destructive weapons thousands of miles away, why can't India hit out at one next door?"[7] Global policemen are self-appointed, and there is nothing America can do—short of using force—to prevent other countries from taking on similar roles themselves. This wearing away of state sovereignty would have very harmful results for long-term world stability.

America, as a superpower, will always have an active role to play in international affairs. American economic and diplomatic well-being is implicated in the smooth running of global commerce and government. The United States, however, should not allow its predominant military power to blind it to the fact that its ability to remake the world in its own image is

Peacekeeping's Drain on Military Effectiveness.

One day last fall [2000] in Bosnia, I met a lieutenant in the U.S. Army, a peacekeeper there, who said he worried about America's role in the world. ...The lieutenant was a willing soldier, but somewhat disillusioned. He had been trained as an infantryman to close with the enemy and fight, and instead now found himself doing the work of a street-corner diplomat. It was not just that he felt individually unsuited to the role; he said that the entire brigade, 3,500 strong, had lost its war-fighting ability and would require six months of retraining upon returning home. I was a bit skeptical about that claim, which is often made, but I also knew that it was not entirely without merit. These soldiers had already spent six months in specialized training before coming to Bosnia, during which they had been encouraged to unlearn the standard kill-or-die mentality, and had been allowed to neglect their traditional military skills. The most perishable of those skills did not consist of shooting guns but, rather, involved the complex organizational interactions necessary to coordinate large groups of embattled fighters. In Bosnia the soldiers had indeed been forced to set much of that aside. ...

The Pentagon complains that the number of its overseas "deployments" has tripled in recent years, neglecting to mention that many of the missions are minuscule and consist of sending off just a few instructors or engineers. If they're camped in a hotel for long enough, it counts. Still, the worry about overextension is real, and it reflects one of the stranger ideas of our time — that for the American military the apparently trivial problem of peacekeeping has recently proved to be more difficult even than waging war.

Source: William Langewiesche, "Peace Is Hell," *The Atlantic Monthly*, October 2001.

very limited. America should be very careful of overextending the definition of its vital interests and involving itself in regional affairs that it does not fully understand and certainly cannot control. Benign influence in the world is one thing; heavy-handed intrusion is quite another.

U.S. Security Requires a Strong Nuclear Deterrent

I n 1964, director Stanley Kubrick released an Oscar-nominated black comedy, *Dr. Strangelove, Or: How I Learned to Stop Worrying and Love the Bomb*, which became a cultural icon of the Cold War and the nuclear arms race. The film is a satiric masterpiece. The story begins when a nuclear-armed B-52 bomber on a routine patrol on the fringes of Soviet airspace is suddenly ordered to attack a Soviet military base. It turns out that this attack has been ordered not by the White House, but by a deranged air force officer, "General Jack D. Ripper," who has become convinced that the Soviets are secretly poisoning America's water supply with fluoride—which, by the way, some people really believed in the 1950s. "I can no longer sit back and allow the international Communist conspiracy to sap and impurify all of our precious bodily fluids!" says Ripper to his horrified but powerless second-in-command.[1] When the Pentagon discovers what has happened, the Joint Chiefs of Staff realize that they cannot recall their bomber because the crew has been trained to ignore any mission cancellation signals in case they are a Soviet ruse. Then the sinister national security advisor "Dr. Strangelove," a character loosely based on real-life figures such as ex-Nazi scientist Werner von Braun, who helped create America's space and missile programs, reveals that the Soviets have a Doomsday Machine that will literally destroy the world once they are attacked. The movie ends with a montage of nuclear mushroom clouds as a sentimental ballad from World War II plays.

The movie's resonance with its audience was increased because it came out only a year after the Cuban Missile Crisis, a Cold War standoff between President John F. Kennedy and Soviet leader Nikita Khrushchev that might have ended in a nuclear exchange between the two superpowers. Near disasters such as this, combined with the absurdist mockery of books and films like *Dr. Strangelove*, encouraged many Americans and Western Europeans to demand atomic weapons reduction through groups such as the Campaign for Nuclear Disarmament (CND).

Strangely, the Cold War was finally brought to an end not by nuclear disarmament, but by an *increase* in weapons spending. The Reagan administration's policy of building up America's military strength proved so difficult for the financially weak Soviet Union to match that Mikhail Gorbachev, its leader after 1985, effectively abandoned the arms race and began a program of political and economic reforms—"Glasnost" and "Perestroika"— that eventually led to the collapse of the Communist bloc. However much the U.S. policy of nuclear deterrence might have frightened and even appalled some, it ultimately paid off: The Soviet Union and its satellite dictatorships fell apart, to be replaced by new, generally more democratic regimes. The world was not destroyed and, in fact, emerged from the Cold War a better, freer place. *Dr. Strangelove* was wrong: It may be mad to "love the bomb," but it *is* possible to come to terms with it and to use its deterrence power effectively. Today, just as in the

Cold War era, the nuclear arsenal is still a vital part of the apparatus keeping America and its allies safe.

> • **Why do you think the Soviet Union was willing to destroy itself financially in order to keep pace with American military progress? Do you think any nation would do the same thing today?**

Nuclear Missiles Will Always Be a Necessary Weapon of Last Resort

The rationale behind nuclear deterrence has a brutal quality to it that makes many people instinctively uncomfortable. Even the name used to describe Cold War deterrence theory, "Mutually Assured Destruction," has an acronym—MAD—that suggests that only the certifiably insane would support it. After all, the

Extracts from the National Institute for Public Policy's "Rationale and Requirements for U.S. Nuclear Forces and Arms Control."

Nuclear weapons come with positive and negative attributes. What are additional plausible priorities when considering how U.S. nuclear forces may support these goals in the context of a dynamic strategic environment? In particular, U.S. nuclear weapons may be necessary to:

- Deter escalation by regional powers to the use of WMD [weapons of mass destruction], while the United States is defeating those powers in the conduct of a conventional war in defense of U.S. allies and security partners.
- Deter regional powers or an emerging global power from WMD or massive conventional aggression against the United States or its allies.
- Prevent catastrophic U.S. and allied wartime losses in a conventional war.
- Provide unique targeting capabilities in support of possible U.S. deterrence and wartime goals.
- Enhance U.S. influence in crises.

theory is rather stark. It argues that no two powers armed with a large stockpile of nuclear weapons will ever attack one another because each knows that it will automatically be obliterated by the counter-barrage from the other side. No sneak attack will ever be "sneaky" enough in an age of radar and satellite advance-warning systems, and even the fiercest missile assault will not reach its target before the enemy's own weapons have been launched. MAD gambles, in effect, on the belief that no country wants to invite its own annihilation. Half a century of self-restraint on the part of the United States and the former Soviet Union seems to have proven the theory accurate. However vicious the conflicts became between the two superpowers, the two nations were never seriously tempted to use atomic weapons because the consequences were so obviously catastrophic. MAD is not the manifesto of lunatics but a fresh breath of sanity.

- **What examples from history can you think of in which nations built up their military power in an attempt to prevent war? How have nuclear weapons been a more successful deterrent than conventional weapons?**

MAD is not even a particularly new theory, either. For centuries, nations relied upon a balance of military forces to deter their aggressive neighbors. The reason that traditional deterrence of this kind was often unsuccessful was that, with conventional weapons, there was always a margin of possible victory. No matter how large the enemy's army or navy, there was always the temptation to launch an attack that might succeed by luck or skill. When two powers face off with massive arsenals of nuclear missiles, however, it is impossible for either of them to win. Atomic weapons are so devastating that the only conceivable outcome of such a war is the ruin of both sides. That is why, paradoxically, it is safer for the United States and Russia to keep larger rather than smaller nuclear stockpiles. Although arms reduction can be a useful way of defusing international tension, it should not be allowed to undermine the logic of MAD, for if

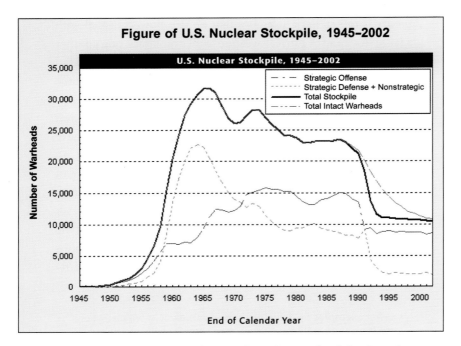

Figure of U.S. Nuclear Stockpile, 1945–2002

Despite arguments against the continued growth of the American arsenal, as this graph demonstrates, the size of the U.S. nuclear stockpile has actually shrunk over the years since around 1970, after an enormous increase during the decades immediately after the end of World War II.

one country's retaliatory power were to shrink too much, its rivals might come to the dangerous conclusion that they could survive an exchange of missiles and so "win" a nuclear war.

> • **Do you think the threat that nuclear weapons might be used would be as powerful if the world had not seen the devastation such weapons cause in the bombings of Hiroshima and Nagasaki in World War II? Under what circumstances do you think the United States might be able to justify the use of nuclear weapons against an enemy?**

The United States and its allies are not committed to avoiding the use of nuclear weapons under every possible wartime circumstance, of course. They maintain a "flexible response" policy, meaning that they reserve the right to the nuclear option if the situation demands but won't necessarily use it. In practice, the United States would employ atomic weapons only in a truly desperate scenario, either because it was itself under attack from Weapons of Mass Destruction (WMD) or because its conventional land, sea, and air forces were unable to defend a vital strategic interest. The point about flexible response—also sometimes known as *calculated ambiguity*—is not that America is eager to use its nuclear arsenal; after all, it abstained from doing so during all of its Cold War battles, including the Vietnam War. By keeping its potential enemies guessing, though, it can maintain a powerful, credible deterrence, and so avoid the risk of war in the first place. As President George W. Bush argued in outlining his future defense policy in 2003, nuclear weapons are necessary because they force potential enemies to consider their actions thoroughly before launching an attack against the United States.[2]

Proliferation of Nuclear Weapons Means Our Deterrent Is All the More Vital

- **How does the proliferation of nuclear weapons to additional nations make the world more dangerous? Are certain nations more "trustworthy" than others?**

In the bipolar Cold War, the nuclear balance of terror was a relatively straightforward strategic problem. True, nations besides the United States and the Soviet Union possessed atomic weapons—Great Britain, France, and China—but the first two were part of the Western NATO alliance, and the last heeded the conservative rules of the so-called "nuclear club." Since the 1990s, however, the club has unexpectedly acquired new and less predictable members. In May 1998, India conducted five under-ground tests of nuclear devices, which its neighbor Pakistan immediately countered with a similar series of explosions. This was a shock to the international community, since both countries previously had denied possessing or wishing to build atomic weapons. As India and Pakistan continue to feud for possession of the disputed Kashmir province, the thought of a frontier clash spilling over into full-scale armed conflict, and eventually an exchange of nuclear missiles, is a terrifying possibility. Even more worrying are the persistent rumors that rogue nations such as Iran and North Korea are close to obtaining nuclear technology. It now looks as though Iraqi dictator Saddam

Extracts from the CIA's 2001 Report to Congress on the Acquisition of Technology Relating to Weapons of Mass Destruction.

Iran is vigorously pursuing programs to produce indigenous WMD—nuclear, chemical, and biological—and their delivery systems. . . . Despite Iran's status in the Treaty on the Nonproliferation of Nuclear Weapons (NPT), the United States is convinced Tehran is pursuing a nuclear weapons program. . . .

North Korea probably has produced enough plutonium for at least one, and possibly two, nuclear weapons. Spent fuel rods canned in accordance with the 1994 Agreed Framework contain enough plutonium for several more weapons. . . .

Libya continues to develop its nuclear infrastructure. The suspension of UN sanctions has provided Libya the means to enhance its nuclear infrastructure through foreign cooperation and procurement efforts. Tripoli and Moscow continued talks on cooperation at the Tajura Nuclear Research Center and a potential power reactor deal. Such civil-sector work could present Libya with opportunities to pursue technologies that also would be suitable for military purposes. . . . Libya's continuing interest in nuclear weapons and ongoing nuclear infrastructure upgrades raises concerns. . . .

Nuclear, chemical, biological, and ballistic missile–applicable technology and expertise continues to gradually disperse worldwide. Nuclear fuel-cycle and weapons-related technologies have spread to the point that from a technical standpoint, additional proliferators may be able to produce sufficient fissile material for a weapon and to develop the capability to weaponize it.

Hussein did not possess an advanced nuclear program, partly because his earlier plans were disrupted by a 1981 Israeli attack on Iraq's main atomic research center. The Iranians and North Koreans, on the other hand, who have suffered less external interference, may have progressed much further.

> • **How severe do you think an attack would have to be for the United States to actually put its nuclear arsenal to use? Does the fact that a nuclear retaliation is highly unlikely make enemies less intimidated by the United States?**

This is an alarming prospect, but it underlines more than ever the need for the United States to retain its nuclear deterrent. There is some argument about whether the traditional MAD policy will be enough to keep unstable regimes in check. This is driving the debate over the costs and benefits of an additional Ballistic Missile Defense (BMD) program. Even if the nuclear deterrent is not a sufficient condition to ward off such aggressors, however, it remains a very necessary part of the defense equation. Would-be assailants need to understand that any use of WMD against the United States or its allies would result in decisive and devastating retaliatory action—psychological "shock and awe," but on a vastly larger scale than anything seen in Iraq in 2003. There are other useful actions that America can take to suppress the proliferation of nuclear arms, such as engaging in greater international cooperation policing the illicit trade in atomic equipment and research materials. Despite these tactics, the final guarantor of U.S. security in this increasingly dangerous world must rest with the homeland's nuclear arsenal.

The Benefits of Possessing Nuclear Weapons Outweigh the Risks

Critics sometimes argue that the mere possession of nuclear weapons is too dangerous to justify because the risk that they might be accidentally fired or exploded, thus setting off a potentially apocalyptic war by mistake, outweighs their usefulness. It is true that during the Cold War both sides made clumsy errors in handling their nuclear weapons that risked catastrophe. Although we know more about blunders made by the United States than by the Soviets, it is probably fair to guess that the Soviet Union had its share of close calls, too. The United States military learned from its earlier procedural faults, though. Today, the process for authorizing and launching ICBMs and other nuclear weapons is exhaustive and excludes many of the dangerous loopholes that existed during the Cold War period.

> • **Does the possibility that an error might lead to massive destruction mean that the United States should not maintain its huge arsenal? Do you think the benefits outweigh the risks?**

Of course, in an imperfect world, no one can ever absolutely guarantee that a mistake will not happen. People, however, accept calculated risks in every aspect of their lives. The question we must ask ourselves is not whether we can eliminate any possibility of error—for that is inherently impossible—but whether the tiny risk of an atomic weapons accident outweighs the much larger risk of military aggression by a hostile foreign power in the absence of an American nuclear deterrent. There is no 100 percent fail-safe solution. There is only the balancing of a very unlikely scenario against an all-too-likely one. It is folly to behave as if nuclear weapons can be wished away on a whim; they are a fact, and we deal with them best by realistically assessing their costs and benefits rather than pretending that their existence is optional.

A Nuclear Deterrent Is Necessary to Defend Democracy

Where would we now be without our unloved nuclear guardians? The threat from the Soviet Union and its former allies in the Warsaw Pact dissipated so quickly after 1991 that it is difficult to recall just how recently the whole of NATO in Western Europe was menaced by the Soviet Union. There was a very real threat that the

Soviets would launch a preemptive strike that used their large advantage in conventional ground and air forces. "The goal of Soviet military strategy in Europe was a quick victory over NATO in a non-nuclear war," says one study. "Soviet military strategists planned to defeat NATO decisively before its political and military command structure could consult and decide how to respond to an attack."[3] It is also evident from records of the former Communist East German state that "the preliminary and advanced training of the military leadership, the training of troops and staffs, and the infrastructure, personnel and communications of the Warsaw Pact were all aimed at preparing for a rapid attack deep into France."[4] Clearly, the Soviet threat was far from imaginary. The only line of effective deterrence to this Communist takeover of the European heartland was, ultimately, the American nuclear arsenal. Would democracy have triumphed in the East if the Soviet Union had not been prevented from attempting a first strike against NATO during the 1960s and 1970s? It may not have been popular, but MAD was the best argument the West possessed to dissuade the Soviets from such a frightening scheme—and the power of its logic has not diminished with time.

———————————————

The government's most recent review of its nuclear deterrent strategy argues that "Nuclear weapons play a critical role in the defense capabilities of the United States, its allies and friends. They provide credible military options to deter a wide range of threats, including WMD and large-scale conventional military force."[5] Despite the many changes that are taking place in the world today, this role will remain constant. We cannot un-invent or wish away nuclear weapons, however much we might want to. They are a permanent part of our lives, and rather than simply recoil from them in horror, we have to learn to control and harness their critical deterrent value. In this way, we may be able to avoid ever seeing them used again.

America Should Reduce Its Nuclear Arsenal

n June 1947, the *Bulletin of the Atomic Scientists,* a journal published by the nonprofit Educational Foundation for Nuclear Science, ran on its front cover the striking picture of a "Doomsday Clock," with its minute hand pointing to seven minutes before midnight—meaning nuclear Armageddon. The clock was intended to provide a graphic warning about the dangers of Cold War confrontation between the United States and the Soviet Union, and the positioning of the original minute hand was somewhat arbitrary. Still, it proved to be such an arresting image that the *Bulletin* retained the clock and, over the years, altered its time to reflect increases or decreases in the apparent likelihood of a nuclear war. For example, in 1949 when the Soviet Union exploded its first atomic bomb, the minute hand was moved up to five minutes to midnight. Throughout the Cold War, the *Bulletin's* staff continued to tweak the clock, depending on the state of superpower tensions. Sometimes, as in 1972, when the first Strategic Arms Limitations Talks (SALT) between East and West began, they turned the clock back; but at other times, such as in the early 1980s, when suspicion between the two sides was at its height, the minute hand moved inexorably forward. Only in 1988, as the Cold War began to thaw, did the clock's minute hand return to a safer position, and by 1991, it had retreated to the unprecedented distance of 17 minutes to midnight.

> • **How severe do you think the threat of nuclear war is today? Do you think nuclear war is more or less likely than it was during the Cold War period?**

Less than a decade later, however, in February 2002, the clock had returned to the disturbing position of seven minutes to midnight—exactly where it had begun 55 years before. What had caused such a turnaround? The Cold War was, after all, over. The *Bulletin* editors explained their reasoning:

> Too little progress on global nuclear disarmament; growing concerns about the security of nuclear weapons materials worldwide; the continuing U.S. preference for unilateral action rather than cooperative international diplomacy; U.S. abandonment of the Anti-Ballistic Missile (ABM) Treaty . . . the crisis between India and Pakistan; [and] terrorist efforts to acquire and use nuclear and biological weapons.[1]

The *Bulletin* did recognize some welcome developments, such as President Bush's decision the previous year to reduce the number of "operationally deployed strategic warheads" in the U.S. arsenal. Otherwise, though, it was pessimistic about the prospects of maintaining peace in a world where thousands of ICBMs remain on hair-trigger alert, ready to be fired at a moment's notice.

> • **Is protecting American citizens from the threat of outside aggression more or less important than providing for their basic needs at home? How do you think the government should spend its money, given the global climate today?**

A 1998 report by the Brookings Institute estimated that, since the construction of the first atomic bombs during World War II, the U.S. federal government has spent approximately $5.5 trillion on nuclear weapons—a larger sum than was expended during the same period on education, social services, agriculture, community and regional development, law enforcement, and energy production combined.[2] Have American citizens received value for that money? Can a defense that keeps us on the perpetual brink of apocalyptic war really be described as providing "security" for the United States? As the Doomsday Clock suggests, the potential for this wildly expensive weapons system to precipitate global disaster in a terrifyingly short space of time is ever-present.

MAD Is an Inherently Immoral Doctrine

The keystone of the continued justification for the U.S. nuclear deterrent is MAD, or Mutually Assured Destruction. We have become so familiar with its gloomy logic that even the acronym no longer inspires any comment, and yet, MAD *is* mad; in fact, it is utterly insane. It requires us to believe that deliberately destroying much of the world is a rational military option, and that we can take it upon ourselves to hold planet Earth's future in jeopardy for the sake of our own perceived security needs. As one writer puts it, "How can a nation live with its conscience and know that it is preparing to kill twenty million children in another nation if the worst should come to the worst?"[3] That estimate is probably at the conservative end of the scale. Should MAD ever be triggered, the outcome is more likely to be the annihilation of billions of people and the collapse of human civilization as we know it. The scale of responsibility this suggests is so staggering that it is scarcely any wonder people have difficulty conceiving of it, and yet Americans have been supporting the policy of MAD now for decades with startling little public debate.

> • **Can you think of any situation in which you would consider the use of nuclear weapons morally justifiable?**

The carrying out of a war in a just fashion is known in Latin as *jus in bello*. One of its traditional principles is that of "proportionality." This means that, in order to remain just, an attacker must only use force that is in proportion to the original offense. So, for example, a country that is involved in a minor conflict with its neighbor over a disputed piece of land cannot raze the enemy's cities and enslave its people without acting unjustly; that degree of aggression is simply not warranted by the circumstances. Would MAD fit into the judgment of *jus in bello*? It is difficult to see how. What offense could be so severe that it would justify the effective destruction of the world? A full-scale nuclear assault is so out of proportion to any conceivable act that it would *never* be justifiable on any grounds. Whatever MAD's virtues may be, it is morally indefensible.

Our Maintenance of Nuclear Weapons Encourages Their Proliferation

Since 1991, membership in the nuclear club of nations has continued to grow. Most notably, the atomic tests by India and Pakistan in 1998 have made clear that proliferation of nuclear technology across the developing world is now a fact. Proponents of the U.S. nuclear deterrent claim that this makes America's retention of its ICBMs all the more important, given the likely spread of Weapons of Mass Destruction (WMD) throughout Asia and the Middle East in the decades to come. The weakness of that argument, however, is that it ignores the effect that America's weapons arsenal is having on the very problem of nuclear proliferation: U.S. possession of

WMD is *increasing* the likelihood that more and more nations will covet atomic weapons.

The reason for this is that the emphasis the United States places on its deterrent underlines to other world leaders the idea that possession of nuclear weapons is the only way a government can be taken seriously by the leading powers in the international community. An atomic warhead is the necessary key to gain America's interest and respect. It has not escaped the notice of many developing states that the five permanent members of the United Nations Security Council—the members that hold veto rights over all decisions—also happen to be the five original members of the nuclear club. This is far from being a coincidence.

> • **Do you think the possession of nuclear weapons makes a country more respected in the international community? Is that why so many countries want to build such weapons? What other motives might a country have for trying to obtain nuclear technology?**

India and Pakistan's experience is a perfect example. Both countries developed their nuclear programs in secret, and after they revealed that they had produced atomic weapons technology, the initial response from the United States and other Western governments was to condemn the move and introduce a few token sanctions. However, it soon became clear that the two new nuclear club members would not be cajoled into disarming their weapons; they were too strategically important for the United States and its allies to ostracize permanently. India's and Pakistan's status as nuclear powers has been tacitly, if grudgingly, accepted by the United States, and they have acquired a diplomatic prestige that they never enjoyed when they were merely conventionally armed nations. Building an atomic bomb is clearly useful for more than just defense: It brings status as well as security. The only way that the United States can thwart the dangerous temptation to build nuclear weapons is to encourage as many nations as possible to reduce their nuclear arsenals—partly by the

The World's Nuclear Arsenals

	Country	Suspected Strategic Nuclear Weapons	Suspected Nonstrategic Nuclear Weapons	Suspected Total Nuclear Weapons
	China	250	120	400
	France	350	0	350
	India	60	?	60+?
	Israel	100–200	?	200+?
	Pakistan	24–48	?	24–48
	Russia	~ 6,000	~ 4,000	~10,000
	United Kingdom	180	5	185
	United States	8,646	2,010	10,656

Some observers believe that non-nuclear states work hard to develop nuclear capabilities in hopes of gaining additional international prestige. It seems that respect does come with nuclear weapons. All of the permanent members of the UN Security Council (each of which may veto UN resolutions) — China, France, Russia, Great Britain, and the United States — are nuclear powers. This chart shows the estimated size of the nuclear arsenals of those nations that currently possess atomic weapons.

example of reducing its own—and diminish the cachet associated with WMD.

The Risk of Nuclear Weapons Accidents Is Too Great

The moral argument against MAD is that it is monstrous to contemplate the deliberate destruction of the world out of

Mishaps That Might Have Started Accidental Nuclear War

At 8:50 A.M. on November 9, 1979, duty officers at 4 command centers (NORAD HQ, SAC Command Post, the Pentagon National Military Command Center, and the Alternate National Military Command Center) all saw on their displays a pattern showing a large number of Soviet Missiles in a full scale attack on the U.S.A. During the next 6 minutes emergency preparations for retaliation were made. A number of Air Force planes were launched, including the President's National Emergency Airborne Command Post, though without the President! The President had not been informed, perhaps because he could not be found. No attempt was made to use the hot line either to ascertain the Soviet intentions or to tell the Soviets the reasons for U.S. actions. This seems to me to have been culpable negligence. The whole purpose of the "Hot Line" was to prevent exactly the type of disaster that was threatening at that moment.... The reason for the false alarm was an exercise tape running on the computer system. U.S. Senator Charles Percy happened to be in NORAD HQ at the time and is reported to have said there was absolute panic....

On January 25, 1995, the Russian early warning radars detected an unexpected missile launch near Spitzbergen. The estimated flight time to Moscow was 8 minutes. The Russian President, the Defense Minister, and the Chief of Staff were informed. The early warning and the control and command center switched to combat mode. Within 5 minutes, the radars determined that the missile's impact would be outside the Russian borders. The missile was Norwegian, and was launched for scientific measurements. On January 16, Norway had notified 35 countries including Russia that the launch was planned. Information had apparently reached the Russian Defense Ministry, but failed to reach the on-duty personnel of the early warning system.

Source: Physicians for Global Survival, available online at http://www.pgs.ca/pgs.php/Abolition/64/.

revenge or fear. Perhaps an even more disturbing possibility, however, is that ICBMs might trigger a nuclear holocaust by accident. Apocalypse could unintentionally come about by human or mechanical error. The Cold War provides several hair-raising examples of near-disastrous mistakes. As one writer explains, "The rising moon was misinterpreted as a missile attack during the early days of long-range radar. A fire at a broken gas pipeline was believed to be enemy jamming by laser of a satellite's infrared sensor when those sensors were first deployed."[4] During the Cuban Missile Crisis in 1962, a bear trying to break through the perimeter fence of a Wisconsin military base triggered a wrongly wired security alarm at a nearby airfield, and the pilots—believing that World War III had started—raced to their nuclear-armed bombers. Only a frantic officer speeding across the runway prevented them from taking off. None of these accidents actually resulted in a nuclear war, but is there any consolation in that? The potential consequences of a blunder of this kind would be so calamitous that *any* risk is arguably too great. Mutually Assured Destruction is not something with which to take gambles.

A Nuclear Deterrent Is Incompatible With Democracy

The U.S. nuclear deterrent is supposedly in place to protect democracy. In what sense, though, could the choice of whether or not to use our nuclear weapons in a time of crisis ever be "democratic"? The idea of popular participation in the major decisions of state is central to the American understanding of what democracy is. The U.S. Constitution requires that the president authorize any declaration of war through Congress, demanding that the people be involved and informed about any decision with such drastic ramifications for the country's future. How could this constitutional provision ever be honored in the event of a nuclear war? As David Krieger puts it, "Will any Congress or Parliament be asked to debate whether nuclear weapons should be used in retaliation? The theory of deterrence does not allow for this; it rather demands sure and swift retribution."[5]

> • **Does the government's ability to use nuclear weapons without the people's consent undermine American democracy? How would the possible use of nuclear weapons differ from the use of traditional military force in this respect?**

This is not just procedural nitpicking; it is a crucial point about the transfer of power from the people to the government. If American citizens are not going to be consulted about the decision to use nuclear weapons, then essentially, the most important choice the United States ever makes will be in the hands of a tiny group of politicians and technocrats who cannot be held responsible for their actions. Considering that the future of the human race will hang in the balance of such a decision, this is an alarmingly passive surrender of authority. The nuclear

THE LETTER OF THE LAW

Extracts from the 1970 Treaty on the Non-Proliferation of Nuclear Weapons.

Each nuclear-weapon State Party to the Treaty undertakes not to transfer to any recipient whatsoever nuclear weapons or other nuclear explosive devices or control over such weapons or explosive devices directly, or indirectly; and not in any way to assist, encourage, or induce any non-nuclear-weapon State to manufacture or otherwise acquire nuclear weapons or other nuclear explosive devices, or control over such weapons or explosive devices....

Each non-nuclear-weapon State Party to the Treaty undertakes not to receive the transfer from any transferor whatsoever of nuclear weapons or other nuclear explosive devices or of control over such weapons or explosive devices directly, or indirectly; not to manufacture or otherwise acquire nuclear weapons or other nuclear explosive devices; and not to seek or receive any assistance in the manufacture of nuclear weapons or other nuclear explosive devices....

deterrent is an inherently undemocratic implement. There was a notorious episode during the Vietnam War in which an American press officer defended the burning of a Vietnamese community by saying, "We had to destroy the village in order to save it."[6] The proponents of MAD are essentially defending the same idea on a larger scale—that we can destroy the world in order to save American democracy.

The U.S. nuclear deterrent is both morally unjustifiable and a handicap to the country's national security. It is illogical to believe that possessing weapons that can instantly wipe out thousands of years of human progress is ever safe. Far from guaranteeing the nation's defense, nuclear missiles actually endanger us by encouraging the spread of atomic weapons technology throughout the world. The only sensible course is to reduce the United States' nuclear arsenal to as small a size as possible, through multilateral disarmament agreements with Russia and China. The ultimate aim—though it may not be possible for generations to come—should be the outlawing of nuclear weapons entirely.

America Needs a Ballistic Missile Defense Shield

At 10:40 P.M. on Saturday July 14, 2001, a Minuteman II intercontinental ballistic missile (ICBM) capable of carrying a 1.2 megaton nuclear warhead—a weapon many times more powerful than the atomic bombs that destroyed the Japanese cities of Hiroshima and Nagasaki in 1945—was launched from Vandenberg Air Force Base near Los Angeles and soared thousands of miles per hour high into the upper atmosphere over the Pacific. About 20 minutes later, almost 5,000 miles (8,047 kilometers) and an ocean away at the Kwajalein Atoll in the Marshall Islands chain, a 55-foot-long (17-meter-long) "Kill Vehicle" designed to track, intercept, and destroy the Minuteman was also launched into Earth's thermosphere, toward the fringes of outer space. Traveling with a combined collision speed of about 16,500 miles

(26,554 kilometers) per hour, the two projectiles hurtled toward one another, the Minuteman using a decoy balloon to try to disguise its true location. Despite this tactic, the interceptor's sophisticated targeting equipment was able to locate and lock onto the real ICBM, and at 11:09 P.M.— just eight minutes after the second launch from Kwajalein— the two smashed into one another 140 miles (225 kilometers) above Earth. The Kill Vehicle's explosive payload detonated and smashed both projectiles to dust in a brilliant flash of light.[1]

> • **Do you think building a missile defense shield is a good way to prevent nuclear war? Would such a defense allow the United States to stop producing additional nuclear weapons?**

The test's success was a dramatic vindication of the practicality of a Ballistic Missile Defense (BMD) system for the United States, a system that would seek out and destroy incoming ICBMs before they could deliver their nuclear warheads against America's cities. Critics of the BMD vision had

THE LETTER OF THE LAW

The National Missile Defense Act of 1999.

It is the policy of the United States to deploy as soon as is technologically possible an effective National Missile Defense system capable of defending the territory of the United States against limited ballistic missile attack (whether accidental, unauthorized, or deliberate) with funding subject to the annual authorization of appropriations and the annual appropriation of funds for National Missile Defense. . . . It is the policy of the United States to seek continued negotiated reductions in Russian nuclear forces.

[Signed by:] Speaker of the House of Representatives,
Vice President of the United States, and President of the Senate

long charged, among other complaints, that the technology necessary to make missile interception a reality was simply too unreliable—a dreamy fantasy that had more in common with the space-opera of the *Star Wars* movies than with hard-headed science. Earlier demonstrations of the Kill Vehicle technology had been embarrassing public failures and had reinforced this skepticism. The triumph of the Kwajalein-Vandenberg test in July 2001, however, along with a series of equally successful follow-up trials throughout the following year, dispelled much of the uncertainty surrounding BMD and opened the way for the Bush administration's full-fledged endorsement of strategic missile defense. In anticipation of this, the U.S. government in December 2001 announced that it was abandoning its 30-year-old agreement with the former Soviet Union, now the Russian Republic, not to construct missile defenses.

A year later, on December 17, 2002, President Bush formally ordered the creation of a limited BMD network across the Western Hemisphere by 2004 at the latest, with up to 20 ground-based interceptors in California and Alaska and a further array of sea-based Kill Vehicles at key offshore locations. The president also made it clear that this was potentially just the start of a much more elaborate scheme in years to come, with many other elements, including laser-beam weapons and intricate satellite-based sensor and tracking systems. "[T]hese capabilities will add to America's security and serve as a starting point for improved and expanded capabilities," he said.[2] This decision, while less ambitious than the all-encompassing "Strategic Defense Initiative" proposals of President Ronald Reagan in the 1980s, was a welcome one, for it finally committed the United States to the development and deployment of a long-overdue and much-needed shield against the horrors of nuclear attack.

The successful test of a missile interceptor over the Pacific Ocean in November 2001 encouraged renewed efforts to develop a ballistic missile defense system. In this photograph taken a few days after the test, Major General Ronald Kadish, director of the Ballistic Missile Defense Organization, gives a press conference while standing beside the type of Killer Vehicle nose cone to be used in the proposed system.

Extracts from President Bush's Statement on Missile Defense, December 17, 2002.

When I came to office, I made a commitment to transform America's national security strategy and defense capabilities to meet the threats of the 21st century. Today, I am pleased to announce that we will take another important step in countering these threats by beginning to field missile defense capabilities to protect the United States, as well as our friends and allies. . . .

September 11, 2001 underscored that our Nation faces unprecedented threats, in a world that has changed greatly since the Cold War. To better protect our country against the threats of today and tomorrow, my Administration has developed a new national security strategy, and new supporting strategies for making our homeland more secure and for combating weapons of mass destruction. Throughout my Administration, I have made clear that the United States will take every necessary measure to protect our citizens against what is perhaps the gravest danger of all: the catastrophic harm that may result from hostile states or terrorist groups armed with weapons of mass destruction and the means to deliver them. Missile defenses have an important role to play in this effort. . . .

I have directed the Secretary of Defense to proceed with fielding an initial set of missile defense capabilities. We plan to begin operating these initial capabilities in 2004 and 2005, and they will include ground-based interceptors, sea-based interceptors, additional Patriot (PAC-3) units, and sensors based on land, at sea, and in space.

Because the threats of the 21st century also endanger our friends and allies around the world, it is essential that we work together to defend against them. The Defense Department will develop and deploy missile defenses capable of protecting not only the United States and our deployed forces, but also our friends and allies.

The new strategic challenges of the 21st century require us to think differently, but they also require us to act. The deployment of missile defenses is an essential element of our broader efforts to transform our defense and deterrence policies and capabilities to meet the new threats we face. Defending the American people against these new threats is my highest priority as Commander-in-Chief, and the highest priority of my Administration.

Old Ideas for a New World Order

Although the system of Ballistic Missile Defense now being built in the United States depends upon hi-tech equipment unavailable before the twenty-first century, the essential concepts of BMD actually stretch back to the pre-missile age of manned strategic bomber aircraft. Ever since the introduction of military aviation in World War I (1914–1918), nations have tried to protect themselves from the threat of aerial bombardment. In the 1930s, British scientists developed a system called "Radio-Direction-Finding"—later known more popularly as "radar"—that allowed the United Kingdom to set up a nationwide grid of early-warning stations that could detect incoming enemy bombers and alert the defending fighter squadrons to intercept them. During the Battle of Britain in the summer of 1940, when Great Britain stood virtually alone against Adolf Hitler's Nazi Germany, it was this radar system that saved England from invasion.

> • **Would a formal treaty preventing the use or production of nuclear weapons be as effective as a physical shield against missiles? What if scientists could not guarantee that the shield would work, just as diplomats could not guarantee that all nations would obey the treaty?**

Later in the war, however, when the Nazis developed supersonic unmanned weapons, traditional radar defenses proved useless. This was particularly true against the German "V-2" rocket, the forerunner of all subsequent ballistic missiles, both American and Soviet. Fortunately, the Nazi regime collapsed before the power of the V-2 could be fully realized. Neither the West nor the Soviets, though, could come up with a defense system that would stop the other side's nuclear-armed missiles. Cold War diplomacy focused instead on the sinister logic of Mutual Assured Destruction—

MAD—rather than a more proactive way of blocking missile attack. Indeed, both sides became so convinced that MAD was the only way to ensure peaceful parity and that a practical BMD system was next-to-impossible to build that, in 1972, the United States and the Soviet Union signed the Anti-Ballistic Missile Systems (ABM) Treaty. In it, each side forswore the creation of any kind of coordinated missile defense. Still, each country did leave open the option of withdrawing from the treaty after a six-month notification period if it felt that circumstances warranted such a move.

BMD Will Reduce Nuclear Proliferation and Stabilize International Relations

The threat of Mutual Assured Destruction kept the peace between the two superpowers for half a century. Why, then, can it not do the same in the post–Cold War world? Why did the United States let the ABM Treaty lapse now that cooperation between the world's two nuclear giants is more important than ever?

To answer the second question first, it is not even clear if the ABM Treaty was still technically valid after the collapse of the Communist Soviet Union in 1991. Since only one of its signatories (the United States) remained in being ten years later, it was not clear whether the United States was obliged to withdraw from the treaty when the government of former Soviet leader Leonid Brezhnev, who had signed the agreement, had already ceased to exist. Regardless of the legal niceties, the fact is that Russian President Vladimir Putin accepted the death of the ABM Treaty in 2002 with only muted dissent. Although he argued that the American withdrawal was "an erroneous decision," he did not believe that it would seriously affect relations between Russia and the United States.[3]

- **How has the ending of the Cold War changed the relationship between the United States and the former Soviet Union? Do you think the United States made the right decision in pulling out of the ABM Treaty?**

The reason for this was simple. Putin was aware that, in the event of a full-scale nuclear war with the United States, Russia still possesses more than enough missiles to penetrate the American defense shield envisioned under current BMD proposals. Although the Strategic Defense Initiative (SDI) proposed by President Reagan in the 1980s was supposed to ward off a massive Soviet threat, the Bush administration's more limited (and more realistic) system will not be able to do this. Ultimately, the ending of the ABM Treaty will mean little to the military relationship between the two former superpowers, at least for the foreseeable future, because even if America's BMD program works exactly to plan, it can still be swamped by an enormous nuclear attack. The logic of MAD between the former Cold Warriors remains unaffected.

- **Do you think the existence of a missile defense system would make other nations less eager to build nuclear arsenals of their own? Or do you think they would continue to build weapons and also try to create their own missile defense at the same time?**

The effect of a ballistic missile defense on the overall international situation also will reduce nuclear proliferation and arms development in smaller members of the nuclear club, such as the People's Republic of China, which does not possess the same levels of weapons stocks as Russia. Since the Chinese would be unable to breach an American missile defense shield without a massive and unrealistic expansion of their nuclear arsenal, there will be little point in their continuing to hoard expensive and now strategically useless weapons of mass destruction. Hopefully, they will be encouraged to spend their resources in more peaceful ways, such as commerce or industrial development—something that will benefit everyone in the world.

MAD Will Not Work Against Rogue Nations and Terrorists

The other countries that will be most affected by BMD are those with tiny or potential nuclear arsenals. This is particularly true of such rogue nations as North Korea and Iran, which might also cooperate with terrorist groups in sharing nuclear missile technology. These states do not possess nearly enough weapons to overwhelm an American BMD shield. Why would these countries be undeterred by MAD from attacking the United States? After all, any use of nuclear missiles against the United States or its close allies would be met with an immediate, devastating counterattack. Surely, one might argue, common sense would deter these states from launching such a suicidal blow without the unnecessary extra expense of BMD.

> • **How does the threat posed by a rogue nation or terrorist leader differ from the traditional threat of invasion by a foreign power? What steps might the United States take to respond to this new type of enemy?**

The problem with this line of thinking is that it assumes that rogue nations are led by politicians with the same rational instinct for self-preservation as most "normal" governments. That may not be the case. Even at the height of Cold War tension, the United States could take it for granted that the Soviet Union shared with it "well informed decision makers, a prevalent rationality on both sides, a degree of mutual familiarity, effective channels of communication, and leaders who [were] sensitive to cost and risk."[4] Neither side was going to take action that would clearly lead to its own destruction. Can the same be said for unstable, isolated dictators who show little interest in the well-being of their country's people, or religious zealots fired by the passions of martyrdom? The self-immolation of the September 11 hijackers is the most dramatic example of enemies who care nothing for their own survival. Saddam Hussein's behavior before the Gulf War of 1990–1991 might also be considered. Once it was clear that the West was determined to remove Iraq from Kuwait by force if necessary, the rational thing for Hussein to do would have been to stage a guarded retreat. Instead, he simply ignored the reality facing him, egging on a war he could not possibly win and that easily might have led to his downfall. This was not the behavior of a coherent statesman. If someone as unpredictable as Saddam Hussein possessed a nuclear missile, might he not have been tempted to destroy New York or Washington, D.C., in a fit of savage revenge, even if this would have sealed his own fate? Without BMD, there would be nothing that America could do to prevent such a catastrophe. MAD still has an important role to play in balancing American and Russian power, but only a missile defense can neutralize the danger from other hostile members of the nuclear club.

BMD Will Prevent Nuclear Blackmail

Of course, rogue dictators and terrorists are well aware of this terrible dilemma facing the United States. And, in the absence of a ballistic missile defense, they might—if they could obtain the necessary nuclear materials, something that is becoming easier each year—play a deadly game of bluff against the West. They could blackmail the United States and Western Europe with the risk of destroying a major city and the deaths of millions. Imagine that, when Iraq invaded Kuwait in 1990, Iraqi dictator Saddam Hussein possessed one or more ICBMs capable of reaching American shores.

Hussein could have defied a United Nations response by threatening to launch a strike against an American or European city unless his aggression were left unchallenged. Even if he were bluffing, would any American president be confident enough to risk the lives of so many against the chance—even if it were just a slight chance—that Hussein really meant what he said? It was difficult enough to build an anti-Iraqi coalition in 1990 among states with differing political responses to the invasion of Kuwait. In the face of possible nuclear attack, it would be next to impossible. American military power would be rendered effectively impotent against even a comparatively doubtful threat. Again, only a BMD system could prevent this.

As journalist Christopher Holton wrote for *WorldTribune.com*,

> Such defenses are not intended to defend against a mass ICBM volley from Russia. They are needed to defend against a tyrannist in a rogue nation, especially unbalanced and radical Islamic dictators, launching a few ICBMs against America in an act of ultimate terrorism, aggression or desperation. No longer can we depend on MAD (Mutual Assured Destruction) to deter madmen. . . .[5]

BMD Is a Cheap, Reliable Way of Defending the United States From Missiles

Ballistic missile defense will not make America invulnerable to nuclear attack. There are other means of delivering weapons of mass destruction to their targets, aside from missiles. Just because a security system is not foolproof, however, does not mean it is valueless. We don't stop locking the front door just because the house has a back entrance, too. BMD uses proven, affordable technology to defend the American homeland, U.S. troops overseas, and our allies from the very real threat of a rogue nation's nuclear attack, or diplomatic extortion under such a threat. Now that the knowledge base exists to implement such a defense system, it would be unwise to ignore it on the grounds of false economies or the misconceived notion that change always represents destabilization. BMD would actually strengthen the international order and reduce, not increase, the likelihood of nuclear exchange. Strategic missile defense is an idea whose time has come at last.

A Ballistic Missile Defense Shield Is Useless and Dangerous

Imagine a network of tens of thousands of hi-tech satellites seeded throughout Earth's upper atmosphere, permanently on electronic sentry duty, scanning the flotsam of orbital junk that surrounds the planet for signs of hostile nuclear missiles. Each interceptor, around three feet (one meter) long and 100 pounds (45 kilograms) in weight, is equipped with the latest sensory and communication equipment, and has a silicon brain as powerful as a supercomputer. As soon as enemy ICBMs are detected in flight, the system automatically goes into high alert. The interceptors fire projectiles that home in on the missiles' rocket exhaust trails, deftly avoiding any electronic countermeasures designed to fool them. The giant hunter-killer bullets smash into the ICBMs, destroying the missiles and their lethal atomic warheads long before they can reach their targets. A battery of nuclear weapons thus is

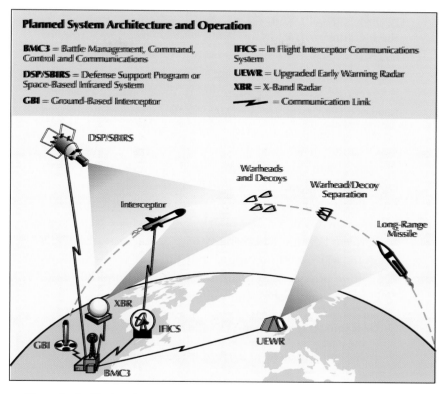

Planned System Architecture and Operation

BMC3 = Battle Management, Command, Control and Communications

DSP/SBIRS = Defense Support Program or Space-Based Infrared System

GBI = Ground-Based Interceptor

IFICS = In Flight Interception Communications System

UEWR = Upgraded Early Warning Radar

XBR = X-Band Radar

━━ = Communication Link

DSP/SBIRS

Warheads and Decoys

Warhead/Decoy Separation

Interceptor

Long-Range Missile

XBR

IFICS

GBI

UEWR

BMC3

Plans for ballistic missile defense systems have been proposed many times since being considered first by the Reagan administration during the 1980s. Critics have long charged that a BMD system would simply be too complex to work effectively. The complexity of a BMD can be seen in this diagram of a system proposed by the Clinton administration in the 1990s.

harmlessly neutralized thousands of miles before approaching American skies.[1]

Sound like science fiction? Unfortunately, that is what the "Brilliant Pebbles" strategic defense concept turned out to be— but not before the U.S. government had spent $4.8 billion trying to turn it into reality. After four years of costly development work, the sum product of the Brilliant Pebbles project, originally unveiled with much fanfare by George H.W. Bush's administration in 1989, was a cone-like lump of electronics about the size of an economy sedan, dumped in a Florida warehouse before being stripped for spare parts. The interceptors, which were supposed to finally realize President Reagan's 1983 vision of a strategic defense system protecting the United States from Soviet nuclear assault, turned out to be vastly more difficult and expensive to produce than their designers had originally promised. Test demonstrations continually flopped; the satellite systems could neither detect their targets nor shoot them down when they were supposed to. Once the Cold War had clearly ended and the technology had proven beyond the capability of U.S. scientists, the whole program was quietly scrapped and the cost written off. As Federation of American Scientists spokesman John Pike said, "Did we get anything for our money? Not that I can detect." [2]

> • **Does the fact that attempts to build missile defense systems in the past have failed mean the United States should stop trying and instead focus defense efforts elsewhere?**

Even past failures like Brilliant Pebbles have not cooled the ardor of the current administration for new ballistic missile defense adventures. Despite the expense of the war on terrorism at home and abroad, in December 2002, President George W. Bush's government committed itself to allotting at least $9 billion a year from the military budget toward new BMD research and development. This will add to the approximately $70 billion that the United States has already spent on missile defense since the idea's inception in the early 1980s—a program that has yet to show any practical results whatsoever. It has been estimated that, if BMD research continues with the present level of government enthusiasm, the final tally may reach $238 billion by 2025. No one knows whether the United States will get anything for its money even by that date. In fact, as experience has shown, BMD is a bottomless money pit. Its technology is dubious at the best of times, and its deployment, far from making America and its allies safer, may actually increase the risk of nuclear conflict. As the antinuclear organization Peace Action of New York argued, "Instead of leading efforts to secure and dismantle nuclear weapons, the Bush Administration wants to build new ones. Spending billions on a missile defense that won't work while building new nuclear weapons will only speed the pace of nuclear proliferation."[3]

A Noble but Flawed Concept

The original motivation behind ballistic missile defense—to protect the United States from the terrifying risk of nuclear

Extracts from the Testimony on BMD before the U.S. Senate Committee on Foreign Relations by the Union of Concerned Scientists.

May 4, 1999, by Dr. David C. Wright.

Both the administration and the Senate have singled out technical readiness as a key criterion that will affect the decision next year on whether or not to begin deployment of a national missile defense system. Is the technology ready to deploy? In this testimony, I will argue the answer is no. Will it be ready to deploy by next summer, when the Deployment Readiness Review is scheduled? Again, I will argue the answer is no.... [T]he type of interceptor the US system will use—a hit-to-kill interceptor that is designed to intercept outside the atmosphere in the vacuum of space—is particularly vulnerable to certain kinds of simple countermeasures. I will not go into detail here, but countermeasures that are technically simple (such as lightweight balloon decoys with the warhead also enclosed in a balloon) can make the system fail catastrophically.

Will these types of simple countermeasures be available to developing countries such as North Korea? Yes....

assault—is, of course, understandable and honorable. The rationale behind Mutual Assured Destruction seems so grim in comparison that few can disagree, at least on an emotional level, with President Reagan's March 23, 1983, address to the American people in which he announced the start of the Strategic Defense Initiative (SDI): "[O]ur only purpose— one all people share—is to search for ways to reduce the danger of nuclear war."[4] It is even possible that the threat of SDI may have forced Soviet leader Mikhail Gorbachev's hand at the summit he attended with Reagan in 1986 in the Icelandic capital of Reykjavik. At the summit, President Reagan convinced the Soviet leader that America's techno-logical lead in missile defense was unassailable, and that only a policy of rapprochement with the West was open to Gorbachev. The Soviet leader responded by hastening a series of reform measures in the Soviet Union that eventually led to its collapse and replacement by a democratic government. In that limited sense, as a form of diplomatic bluff, BMD played a useful historical role.

> • **Would the proposed ballistic missile defense system, originally conceived during the bipolar Cold War era, be as effective a deterrent in the world as it is today?**

Now that the struggle between NATO and the Warsaw Pact is over, though, and Reagan's original vision of an inde-structible shield protecting the United States from a massive Soviet bloc attack has been abandoned as scientifically unfeasible, what is the justification to continue missile defense research? ICBMs are the least of the United States' worries at the beginning of the twenty-first century. The old Cold War nightmare of global nuclear exchange has been replaced by a less technologically sophisticated, but no less terrifying, reality of terrorist violence using relatively simple weapons. The September 11 attacks showed that even box-cutters and small knives can, in a critical situation and in the wrong hands, cause catastrophic damage and loss of life. Al Qaeda terrorists using only old-fashioned explosives and handheld rockets have brought further death, fear, and political turbulence to worldwide targets such as Yemen and Kenya. The United States badly needs to spend its defense dollars to root out and neutralize the immediate threats that face it and its allies, not devote billions to speculative programs that (even if they did work) may serve no useful strategic purpose anyway.

> • **How might the United States defend itself against a smaller-scale attack than those envisioned under current BMD proposals? Are such smaller-scale attacks more likely to occur today? If so, does that make BMD not as useful as it should be?**

Indeed, if a terrorist group such as Al Qaeda or a rogue nation such as North Korea *were* planning to attack the United States with a nuclear weapon, an ICBM would probably be the last type of delivery vehicle that would be chosen. Ballistic missiles, aside from their cost, difficulty to procure, and size, are easily tracked from their launch sites. If, say, some hostile Middle Eastern state chose to fire an ICBM against the United States, it would be a simple matter to trace the source of the launch and respond appropriately. Assuming that enemies of the United States would want, sensibly, to remain anonymous, it would make far more sense to smuggle in a weapon of mass destruction such as an atomic warhead through regular means— by hiding it in a truck and driving it across the Canadian or Mexican border, for example. In an age in which suitcase-sized nuclear weapons are becoming ever more practicable, ICBMs seem to be an unnecessary luxury. The planned BMD system, for all its hi-tech wizardry, would be quite unable to prevent such an attack on a smaller scale. This is the great flaw at the heart of the missile-based strategic defense network: its irrelevancy in the face of the authentic threats to the United States.

BMD Will Increase Nuclear Proliferation and Destabilize International Relations

Missile defense advocates claim that their system would dampen the demand for nuclear weapons development among world nations and contribute to the easing of international tensions. The opposite is more likely to be true.

> • **Do you think the existence of a U.S. BMD would make nations with small numbers of nuclear weapons decide to abandon the idea of attacking the United States, or would it encourage them to continue to build their arsenals, to make a successful attack possible?**

Since the defense shield planned by the Bush administration would only be able to absorb and stop a limited number of hostile nuclear missiles, it would not affect the strategic balance of power between the United States and Russia immediately. However, countries like the People's Republic of China, which has only a relatively small atomic arsenal, would find it more and more difficult to mount a sustainable nuclear challenge to the United States. Proponents of BMD argue that this would discourage China from continuing to develop further ICBMs. This logic, though, seems to fly in the face of the conventional understanding of security relations, which is that, when countries perceive that they are being threatened, they *increase*, not decrease, their military spending and research. The history of the Cold War arms race between the United States and the Soviet Union does not present a very optimistic precedent. Even though both superpowers possessed more than enough nuclear weapons to destroy themselves and their enemy many times over, they continued to press for further weapons production in the belief that this would somehow give them a critical edge against their opponent. A BMD shield would be a spur to even more arms spending, with countries such as China attempting to procure enough missiles to overwhelm the U.S. defense network in time of war. Such spending would only exacerbate existing tensions between nuclear-armed neighbors like India and Pakistan and worsen the overall international situation.

BMD Is Not the Best Deterrent Against Rogue Nations and Terrorists

Another claim made by enthusiasts for missile defense is that it is the only way to ensure protection against terrorists and rogue nations armed with nuclear weapons, because the MAD principle cannot work against such unstable dictators and ideological zealots. The argument is that petty regional tyrannies like North Korea and religiously inspired extremists such as Osama bin Laden are fundamentally different from America's older ideological foes, the Eastern bloc Communists. Unlike those adversaries of an earlier epoch, they lack the necessary rational self-interest to avoid making suicidal attacks on the United States out of sheer hatred. Given the willingness of some Al Qaeda operatives to lay down their lives in atrocities against U.S. targets, it does not appear that American retaliatory threats play an important role in deterring these new enemies from striking against the West.

- **Do you think BMD would be a deterrent against rogue nations or terrorists?**

Still, it is not clear that the leaders of rogue nations or terrorist cells—unlike their rank-and-file followers—actually do treat their own lives with such casual disdain. If he had chosen to do so, Osama bin Laden or his other high-ranking comrades in the Taliban elite could have made a defiant, though suicidal, stand against American forces during Operation Enduring Freedom in Afghanistan in 2001. That they chose not to do this, and, indeed, took every precaution to avoid injury or capture, suggests that even fundamentalist terrorists are not quite as eager to die a martyr's death as they would like to pretend. In truth, people like bin Laden seem just as reluctant to die as everyone else, and given that an easily traced ICBM launch against the United States would, in effect, be a suicide pact, there seems little likelihood that it will happen. MAD, though an unattractive formula, remains a compelling argument against nuclear exchange.

BMD Will Not Prevent Nuclear Blackmail

What about the risk of bluff, though? Without BMD, couldn't a rogue despot or terrorist threaten to attack a Western city with a

THE LETTER OF THE LAW

Extracts from the 1972 Anti-Ballistic Missile Systems Treaty.

The United States of America and the Union of Soviet Socialist Republics ... proceeding from the premise that nuclear war would have devastating consequences for all mankind,

Considering that effective measures to limit anti-ballistic missile systems would be a substantial factor in curbing the race in strategic offensive arms and would lead to a decrease in the risk of outbreak of war involving nuclear weapons,

Proceeding from the premise that the limitation of anti-ballistic missile systems, as well as certain agreed measures with respect to the limitation of strategic offensive arms, would contribute to the creation of more favorable conditions for further negotiations on limiting strategic arms,

Mindful of their obligations under article VI of the Treaty on the Non-Proliferation of Nuclear Weapons,

Declaring their intention to achieve at the earliest possible date the cessation of the nuclear arms race and to take effective measures toward reductions in strategic arms, nuclear disarmament, and general and complete disarmament,

Desiring to contribute to the relaxation of international tension and the strengthening of trust between States,

Have agreed as follows:

- Each Party undertakes to limit anti-ballistic missile (ABM) systems and to adopt other measures in accordance with the provisions of this Treaty.

- Each Party undertakes not to deploy ABM systems for a defense of the territory of its country and not to provide a base for such a defense, and not to deploy ABM systems for defense of an individual region....

nuclear missile unless his demands were met? Even if the challenge were insincere, could a U.S. president placed in such an agonizing position dare take the risk of ignoring it?

> • **How seriously do you think the United States would take a threat posed in the form of nuclear blackmail? Would BMD be a strong enough defense to allow the United States to ignore such threats?**

- Each Party undertakes not to develop, test, or deploy ABM systems or components which are sea-based, air-based, space-based, or mobile land-based.

- Each Party undertakes not to develop, test, or deploy ABM launchers for launching more than one ABM interceptor missile at a time from each launcher, nor to modify deployed launchers to provide them with such a capability, nor to develop, test, or deploy automatic or semi-automatic or other similar systems for rapid reload of ABM launchers....

- This Treaty shall be of unlimited duration.

- Each Party shall, in exercising its national sovereignty, have the right to withdraw from this Treaty if it decides that extraordinary events related to the subject matter of this Treaty have jeopardized its supreme interests. It shall give notice of its decision to the other Party six months prior to withdrawal from the Treaty. Such notice shall include a statement of the extraordinary events the notifying Party regards as having jeopardized its supreme interests.

DONE at Moscow on May 26, 1972.

For the United States of America:
RICHARD NIXON, President of the United States of America.

For the Union of Soviet Socialist Republics:
L. BREZHNEV, General Secretary of the Central Committee of the CPSU.

Such a scenario is indeed frightening. It is far from clear, however, that a working ballistic missile defense shield would do much to stop it. It is an inevitable truth about technology that no system, however well designed or carefully managed, can be relied upon 100 percent. Even with a more sophisticated BMD network than is currently envisaged, the risk would always exist—however slight—that it would fail to operate effectively on the day it was called into use. Under the current, relatively undemanding test conditions of the Kill Vehicles due for installation in Alaska and California by 2004, the success rate has been only a little above 50 percent, and some critics have noted that the tests may have been artificially rigged to make interception easier.[5] Until the moment at which it was required to destroy a genuine ICBM, nobody would really know if an American BMD shield worked effectively. This means that a U.S. government under the threat of nuclear blackmail still would have to face the possibility that its cities would be vulnerable. Perhaps the risk might be tiny, even as low as less than one chance in a hundred. Would that still be a comfortable enough margin of error to accept the possibility of millions of American deaths? Or would the United States have to cave in?

The most effective way to deal with such a terrible quandary is to act as aggressively as possible to prevent nuclear materials falling into the hands of dangerous and unpredictable enemies in the first place. There is little point in building an inherently imperfect system that cannot be relied upon at the moment of crisis anyway.

BMD Is Expensive, Unreliable, and Unnecessary

The United States' recent withdrawal from the 1972 Anti-Ballistic Missile Systems Treaty was an error in itself. It unnecessarily alarmed the Russians and provided an excuse for other international powers to disregard their previous diplomatic commitments to disarmament and nonproliferation.

It would compound this error, however, to begin spending vast sums of money on a missile defense system that is a relic of Cold War thinking, quite irrelevant to the real defense problems that face the nation today. The United States should be using its military budget to buttress security in the homeland and fund antiterrorism measures abroad, not to embark on fantastical science-fiction solutions to an obsolete threat. Ballistic missile defense will only distract the United States from far more compelling concerns.

Conclusion

I n the summer of 1989, as the Soviet bloc began to topple and the Cold War seemed on the brink of ending, commentator Francis Fukuyama wrote a very influential essay called "The End of History." In it, he pointed out that "It is hard to avoid the feeling that something very fundamental has happened in world history. The past year has seen a flood of articles commemorating the end of the Cold War, and the fact that 'peace' seems to be breaking out in many regions of the world." He went on to argue that the post–Cold War environment would represent "an unabashed victory of economic and political liberalism," in which the United States and its Western allies would no longer be presented with any significant ideological opposition of the kind that communism had posed since 1945. Fukuyama was not claiming that the world would enter a permanent realm of peace and security, as some of his critics thought he was suggesting, but he did believe that "large-scale conflict" in the shape of global wars "appear[ed] to be passing from the scene."[1]

Over a decade since its first publication, how does Fukuyama's essay stand up? Did history really "end" in 1991? Did the United States emerge, as he predicted, as the undisputed victor of that process? It is certainly true that American power and influence are at an almost unprecedented height, that our military technology seems to be a quantum leap beyond anything possessed elsewhere in the world, and that people across the globe, particularly in the former Soviet bloc, aspire to U.S. cultural, financial, and political values. Even in the still-formally Communist People's Republic of China, the embrace of American capitalist practices is so complete that it is difficult to see much difference between the Chinese and American economic worldviews, despite the completely different levels of political freedom in each country. So, in one sense, an important theme of history does seem to have ended, and America has emerged triumphant from the process.

> • **How has the rise of Islamic fundamentalism and the use of terrorist tactics changed the way nations must plan their systems of self-defense? How should U.S. military policy be adapted in the face of these new threats?**

However, what Fukuyama did not anticipate was the rise of Islamic fundamentalism in the Middle East and its implications for American security, as shown by the terrible events of September 11, 2001, and by the continuing war on terror. Nor did he appreciate that the countries that in most respects share American values—such as many member-states of the European Union—would come to be increasingly frustrated and disturbed by U.S. policy at the beginning of the twenty-first century. What has become more and more obvious after the optimistic celebrations of the fall of communism is that the post–Cold War world is in many ways a much more complicated place, even for the victor. The United States is no longer faced with a

"Recessional" by Rudyard Kipling.

In 1897, Great Britain was at the height of its power, the greatest military empire on Earth. The poem "Recessional," written that year by Rudyard Kipling, was intended as a warning to his countrymen not to take their future predominance for granted. It remains a valuable warning about the danger of imperial hubris.

God of our fathers, known of old—
Lord of our far-flung battle line—
Beneath whose awful hand we hold
Dominion over palm and pine—
Lord God of Hosts, be with us yet,
Lest we forget—lest we forget!

The tumult and the shouting dies—
The Captains and the Kings depart—
Still stands Thine ancient sacrifice,
An humble and a contrite heart.
Lord God of Hosts, be with us yet,
Lest we forget—lest we forget!

Far-called our navies melt away—
On dune and headland sinks the fire—
Lo, all our pomp of yesterday
Is one with Nineveh and Tyre!
Judge of the Nations, spare us yet,
Lest we forget—lest we forget!

If, drunk with sight of power, we loose
Wild tongues that have not Thee in awe—
Such boastings as the Gentiles use,
Or lesser breeds without the Law—
Lord God of Hosts, be with us yet,
Lest we forget—lest we forget!

For heathen heart that puts her trust
In reeking tube and iron shard—
All valiant dust that builds on dust,
And guarding calls not Thee to guard.
For frantic boast and foolish word,
Thy Mercy on Thy People, Lord!

conventional enemy of the kind that the Soviet Union represented, but it nonetheless must deal with foes as varied in style and tactics as Osama bin Laden and North Korea's dictatorial leader, Kim Jong Il. It must make policy in a world where Weapons of Mass Destruction are continuing to spread, where civil war and revolution disturb regional security, and where the instruments of international law and diplomacy formed after 1945—NATO and the United Nations above all—do not seem properly equipped to tackle today's problems, at least without radical reform. All of the debates presented in this book—the virtues of "global policing," nuclear deterrence, and ballistic missile defense—are reflections of this new complexity.

- **Does the United States have to behave in a certain way now that it is the world's only superpower? How might U.S. actions undermine its influence in world affairs?**

The United States is *primus inter pares*—first among equals— in the international community, but it must not take that precedence for granted. Other nations have held the position before, and lost it—either because of military defeat, or through changing economic realities, or simply because they lost confidence in the wisdom and justice of their own power. In the 2000 presidential election campaign, then–Texas Governor George W. Bush made an important statement about how he thought America's relationship with the world would change during his future presidency. "It really depends upon how our nation conducts itself in foreign policy," he said. "If we're an arrogant nation, they'll resent us. If we're a humble nation but strong, they'll welcome us. . . . [O]ur nation stands alone right now in the world in terms of power. And that's why we've got to be humble and yet project strength in a way that promotes freedom."[2] The problem for the next generation of Americans will be precisely that: how to defend their values and utilize their country's power for the common good, yet avoid the danger of conceit and isolation.

Introduction

1 "Statistics on the War in Iraq as of Wednesday, Apr. 9, 2003," http://vialardi.org/IRAQ/iraq_by_numbers.html

2 Christopher Bellamy, "Military Analysis: Whatever The Conspiracy Theories, The 'Softly-Softly' Plan Seems To Have Worked," *Independent* (UK), April 7, 2003.

3 "Cheney Says War Criticism Is Misguided," Associated Press, April 9, 2003.

4 Statistics from the Center for Defense Information, http://www.cdi.org/issues/wme/oob.html; Sam C. Sarkesian et al., *U.S. National Security: Policymakers, Processes, and Politics* (Boulder: Lynne Reinner, 2002), p. 288.

5 "'Smart' Weapons Pivotal; High-Tech Explosives give Allies Edge", *Atlanta Constitution*, November 21, 2001; "Congress Edges Closer to Deal on Iraq War Money," Associated Press, April 10, 2003.

6 Cynthia A. Watson, *US National Security* (Santa Barbara: ABC-CLIO, 2002), p. 1.

Point: The United States Must Accept the Role of Global Policeman

1 "Americans Fear Bosnia could be Another Vietnam," *Toronto Star*, November 21, 1995, p. 4.

2 "Region's Senators Back Troops; But Republicans Bond and Ashcroft Oppose Clinton's Bosnia Policy," *St. Louis Post-Dispatch*, December 14, 1995, p. 18.

3 "Bosnia Troop Plan Faces Opposition From Illinois", *Chicago Sun-Times*, December 4, 1995, p. 12.

4 William Cohen, "Quadrennial Defense Review," Department of Defense, May 1997.

5 See http://www.freedomhouse.org/media/pressrel/121902.htm

6 Donald Kagan, "Roles and Missions," in John Lehman and Harvey Sicherman, eds., *America the Vulnerable: Our Military Problems and How to Fix Them* (Philadelphia: Foreign Policy Research Institute, 2000), p. 16.

7 The full text of this speech can be found at: http://www.whitehouse.gov/news/releases/2002/06/20020601-3.html

8 PBS, "The Triumph of Evil," http://www.pbs.org/wgbh/pages/frontline/shows/evil/

9 "The Responsibility to Protect," Report of the International Commission on Intervention and State Sovereignty, December 2001. The full text of this report can be found at: http://www.dfait-maeci.gc.ca/iciss-ciise/report2-en.asp

10 "The Burden," *The New York Times Magazine*, January 5, 2003.

Counterpoint: Policing the World Is Beyond Our Means and Not in Our Interests

1 "Tactical Lessons for Peacekeeping: U.S. Multinational Force in Beirut 1982–1984." The full text of this paper can be found at: http://www.fas.org/man/dod-101/ops/docs/baczkow.htm

2 Background on Somalia is available through the CIA World Factbook: http://www.cia.gov/cia/publications/factbook/geos/so.html

3 Nicholas Confessore, "G. I. Woe," *Washington Monthly*, March 2003. The full text of this article can be found at: http://www.washingtonmonthly.com/features/2003/0303.confessore.html

4 Fareed Zakaria, "The Arrogant Empire," *Newsweek*, March 24, 2003. The full text of this article can be found at: http://www.msnbc.com/news/885222.asp?0bl=-0&cp1=1

5 Quoted in Hugh Pope and Peter Waldman, "Past Mideast Invasions Faced Unexpected Perils," *Wall Street Journal*, March 19, 2003.

6 Gary Dempsey, "The Folly of Nation-Building in Afghanistan," October 17, 2001. The full text of this article can be found at: http://www.cato.org/dailys/10-17-01.html

7 Amy Waldman, "India Pressed on Kashmir Attacks," *The New York Times*, April 9, 2003, p. 6.

Point: U.S. Security Requires a Strong Nuclear Deterrent

1 http://www.geocities.com/scifiscripts3/scripts/strangelove.txt

2 http://news1.beograd.com/english/articles_and_opinion/guardian/030109_World_on_path_to_disaster.html

3 Library of Congress Country Study—Soviet Union. Appendix C: The Warsaw Pact. http://lcweb2.loc.gov/frd/cs/soviet_union/su_appnc.html

4 "Warsaw Pact Military Planning in Central Europe: Revelations From the East German Archives." http://www.gwu.edu/~nsarchiv/CWIHP/BULLETINS/b2a3.htm

5 US Nuclear Posture Review, submitted to Congress, 31 December 2001. A copy of extracts from the review can be found at: http://www.globalsecurity.org/wmd/library/policy/dod/npr.htm

Counterpoint: America Should Reduce Its Nuclear Arsenal

1 "Doomsday Clock," *Bulletin of the Atomic Scientists*, http://www.thebulletin.org/media/current.html

2 Stephen Schwartz, "The Hidden Costs of Our Nuclear Arsenal," June 30, 1998. The full text of this report can be found at: http://www.brook.edu/fp/projects/nucwcost/schwartz.htm

3 John Bennett, quoted in Michael Walzer, *Just and Unjust Wars* (New York: Basic-Books, 1992), p. 270.

4 Alan F. Philips, *20 Mishaps That Might Have Started Accidental Nuclear War*. The full text of this report can be found at: http://www.nuclearfiles.org/kinuclearweapons/anwindex.html

5 David Krieger, "Nuclear Weapons Abolition at the Beginning of the 21st Century," c/o Nuclear Age Peace Foundation. See http://www.inesglobal.com/publication/ines_proceedings/Proceed_html/KRIEGER.HTM

6 Available online at http://www.american-partisan.com/cols/yoho/021800.htm.

Point: America Needs a Ballistic Missile Defense Shield

1 "Amid Applause, Caution Urged on Missile Defense," *The New York Times*, July 16, 2001, p. 8.

2 "Antimissile System, In a Limited Form, Is Ordered by Bush," *The New York Times*, December 18, 2002, p. 1.

3 "Facing Pact's End, Putin Decides to Grimace and Bear It", *The New York Times*, December 14, 2001, p. 14.

4 Keith B. Payne, "The Case for National Missile Defense," in John Lehman and Harvey Sicherman, eds., *America the Vulnerable: Our Military Problems and How to Fix Them* (Philadelphia: Foreign Policy Research Institute, 2000), p. 177.

5 Christopher Holton, *World Tribune.com*, http://216.26.163.62/2003/guest_holton_3_03.html

Counterpoint: A Ballistic Missile Defense Shield Is Useless and Dangerous

1 "What's Next for 'Star Wars'? 'Brilliant Pebbles'," *The New York Times*, April 25, 1989, p. C1.

2 "'Star Wars' at Center of New Debate," *Denver Post*, August 25, 1996, p. A1.

3 Peace Action of New York State, http://www.peaceactionnewyorkstate.org/camp_talk_nukes.shtml

4 "President Seeks Futuristic Defense against Missiles," *The Washington Post*, March 24, 1983, p. 1.

5 http://www.ucsusa.org/global_security/missile_defense/page.cfm?pageID=561

Conclusion

1 Francis Fukuyama, "The End of History," Summer 1989. The full text of this essay can be found at: http://www.wku.edu/~sullib/history.htm

2 George W. Bush, Second Presidential Debate, October 11, 2000. The full text of this debate can be found at: http://abcnews.go.com/sections/politics/DailyNews/debate001011_trans_1.html

General

Eland, Ivan. *Putting "Defense" Back into U.S. Defense Policy: Rethinking U.S. Security in the Post–Cold War World.* Westport, CT: Praeger, 2001.

Ikenberry, G. John, ed. *America Unrivaled: The Future of the Balance of Power.* Ithaca, NY: Cornell University Press, 2002.

Lehman, John, and Harvey Sicherman, eds. *America the Vulnerable: Our Military Problems and How to Fix Them.* Philadelphia: Foreign Policy Research Institute, 2000.

Sarkesian, Sam C., et al. *US National Security: Policymakers, Processes, and Politics.* Boulder: Lynne Reinner, 2002.

Schilling, William R., ed. *Nontraditional Warfare: Twenty-First-Century Threats and Responses.* Washington, D.C.: Brassey's, Inc., 2002.

Watson, Cynthia A. *US National Security.* Santa Barbara: ABC-CLIO, 2002.

Zelikow, Philip D., ed. *American Military Strategy: Memos to a President.* New York: W.W. Norton, 2001.

Resources on the Internet

Center for Defense Information

http://www.cdi.org
An independent research organization whose members include retired military officers and knowledgeable civilians who analyze U.S. military issues.

Center for Security Policy

http://www.centerforsecuritypolicy.org
An organization devoted to promoting public knowledge and debate about all aspects of security policy.

DefenseLINK—U.S. Department of Defense

http://www.defenselink.mil
An official Department of Defense site, it provides detailed news about events and policy.

GlobalSecurity.org

www.globalsecurity.org
A research organization that seeks to reduce reliance upon nuclear weapons as part of military policy.

National Security Council

http://www.whitehouse.gov/nsc/
The official website of the National Security Council, the president's main group of advisors on foreign affairs and matters of military security.

Global Policing
Useful Books

Allin, Dana H. *NATO's Balkan Interventions.* New York: Oxford University Press for The International Institute for Strategic Studies, 2002.

Boot, Max. *The Savage Wars of Peace: Small Wars and the Rise of American Power.* New York: Basic Books, 2002.

McInnes, Colin, and Nicholas J. Wheeler, eds. *Dimensions of Western Military Intervention.* Portland, OR: Frank Cass, 2002.

Pollack, Kenneth M. *The Threatening Storm: The Case for Invading Iraq.* New York: Random House, 2002.

Walzer, Michael. *Just and Unjust Wars.* New York: Basic Books, 1992.

Internet Resources on Global Policing

Humanitarianism and War Project

http://hwproject.tufts.edu

Originally a Brown University–based research organization, this group studies the changing world and corresponding security issues and provides information for use in public and governmental debate.

Intervention Magazine

http://www.interventionmag.com

Online publication that publishes articles relating to international military issues, from an anti-intervention standpoint.

Peace Operations Policy Program

http://popp.gmu.edu

Affiliated with George Mason University, this organization explores multinational peacekeeping operations from military, humanitarian, and political angles.

Project on Defense Alternatives

http://www.comw.org/pda/

An organization that studies military affairs and explores options for peaceful resolutions of conflict, arms control, and collective peacekeeping missions.

Nuclear Deterrent
Useful Books

Brembeck, Howard S. *In Search of the Fourth Freedom.* Notre Dame, IN: University of Notre Dame Press, 2000.

Goldblat, Jozef, ed. *Nuclear Disarmament: Obstacles to Banishing the Bomb.* New York: St. Martin's Press, 2000.

Krepon, Michael. *Cooperative Threat Reduction, Missile Defense, and the Nuclear Future.* New York: Palgrave Macmillan, 2003.

Sood, Rakesh, Frank N. von Hippel, and Morton H. Halperin. *The Road to Nuclear Zero: Three Approaches.* Philadelphia: University of Pennsylvania, 1998.

Nuclear Deterrent Resources on the Internet

Center for Nonproliferation Studies

http://cns.miis.edu
An organization devoted to finding ways to combat the spread of weapons of mass destruction.

Nuclear Control Institute

http://www.nci.org
A research organization and advocacy center that focuses on the problems of nuclear proliferation.

NuclearFiles.org

www.nuclearfiles.org
An online guide that explores nuclear issues and the political and ethical problems that occur in the nuclear age.

Union of Concerned Scientists

http://www.ucsusa.org
Organization made up of scientists and interested citizens who research ideas for creating a safe world and promoting clean energy technology.

Ballistic Missile Defense
Useful Books

Graham, Bradley. *Hit to Kill: The New Battle over Shielding America from Missile Attack.* New York: Public Affairs, 2001.

Handberg, Roger. *Ballistic Missile Defense and the Future of American Security: Agendas, Perceptions, Technology, and Policy.* Westport, CT: Praeger, 2002.

Lindsay, James M., and Michael E. O'Hanlon. *Defending America: The Case for Limited National Missile Defense.* Washington, D.C.: Brookings Institution Press, 2001.

Wilkening, Dean A. *Ballistic-Missile Defense and Strategic Stability.* New York: Oxford University Press for the International Institute for Strategic Studies, 2000.

Wirtz, James J., and Jeffrey A. Larsen, eds. *Rockets' Red Glare: Missile Defenses and the Future of World Politics.* Boulder: Westview Press, 2001.

Ballistic Missle Defense Resources on the Internet
Briefing Book on Ballistic Missile Defense
http://www.armscontrolcenter.org/nmd/briefbook02/
A 2002 report from the Center for Arms Contol and Non-Proliferation on issues of military policy.

HighFrontier.org
http://www.highfrontier.org
An educational group that promotes the development of an effective ballistic missile defense.

Missile Defense Agency
http://www.acq.osd.mil/bmdo/
The official government agency whose task is to research defense and deterrence capabilities.

StopStarWars.com (Greenpeace)
http://www.stopstarwars.org
A site dedicated to opposing the creation of a ballistic missle defense system.

Legislation and Treaties

U.S. Constitution, Article I, Section 8, and Article II, Section 2 (War Powers)
Under the Constitution, Congress is given the right to declare war and to deploy the military in the service of the United States. The president is the commander-in-chief of the armed forces, but it is Congress that must make a declaration of war.

War Powers Act (1973)
The president is required to consult Congress in "every possible instance" before American troops are sent into foreign military conflicts. Under this law, the president may deploy troops abroad for no more than 60 days without the approval of Congress.

Massachusetts* v. *Laird, 400 U.S. 886 (1970)
The Supreme Court, over the dissent of three justices, declined to hear a case that challenged President Lyndon Johnson's authority to send troops to Vietnam without a declaration of war by Congress.

Agreement on Measures to Reduce the Risk of Outbreak of Nuclear War Between the United States of America and the Union of Soviet Socialists Republics (1971)
The United States and Soviet Union agreed to implement measures to guard against nuclear accidents within their own arsenals. They also agreed to alert each other in the event of such an accident.

Convention on the Prohibition of the Development, Production and Stockpiling of Bacteriological (Biological) and Toxin Weapons and on Their Destruction (1972)
A group of nations, under United Nations auspices, agreed to take measures to end the production of and prevent the use of chemical and biological weapons.

United Nations Security Council Resolution 1199 (1998)
The United States and a coalition of allies working together as a combined UN force condemned the violence in Kosovo and agreed to provide peacekeeping assistance to the region.

Executive Order Blocking Property and Prohibiting Transactions With Persons Who Commit, Threaten to Commit, or Support Terrorism (September 24, 2001)
President George W. Bush issued an executive order in response to the terrorist attacks of September 11, 2001, that blocked the financial transactions of anyone connected to terrorist activity.

First Resolution of the 56th UN General Assembly (2001)
The United Nations passed a resolution condemning terrorism in response to the attacks against the United States on September 11, 2001.

Joint Resolution 23 (September 13, 2001)
The House of Representatives and the Senate passed a resolution authorizing the use of force against the enemies of the United States in response to the terrorist attacks of September 11, 2001.

HR 2888 2001 Emergency Supplemental Appropriations Act for Recovery from and Response to Terrorist Attacks on the United States. (September 14, 2001)

The House of Representatives voted to make additional emergency appropriations available for the funding of antiterrorist measures and recovery efforts.

Treaty Between the United States of America and the Union of Soviet Socialist Republics on the Limitation of Anti-Ballistic Missile Systems (1972)

The United States and Soviet Union agreed to limit the extent of any potential antiballistic missile systems they might build.

The Roosevelt Corollary (1904)

President Theodore Roosevelt issued an appending statement to the Monroe Doctrine in which he asserted that the United States, as a strong world power, had the right and the obligation to intervene in affairs of the Western Hemisphere when deemed necessary.

Treaty on the Non-Proliferation of Nuclear Weapons (1970)

Signed by members of the United Nations, its objective was to prevent the spread of nuclear weapons and weapons technology, to encourage signers to work together to find peaceful uses of nuclear energy, and to work toward eventual total nuclear disarmament.

The National Missile Defense Act (1999)

The United States outlined its intention to create and deploy a national missile defense system to protect the nation against limited ballistic missile attack (whether accidental, unauthorized, or deliberate).

Concepts and Standards

coalition force
"shock and awe"
"smart" bombs
"Bunker Buster"
Cold War
bipolar world
multipolar world
rogue nations
Weapons of Mass Destruction (WMD)
regime change
asymmetric warfare
overstretch
intercontinental ballistic missile (ICBM)
Nuclear Non-Proliferation Treaty (NPT)
Ballistic Missile Defense (BMD)
peacekeeping missions
global policing
vital interests
preemptive action
isolationism

foreign entanglements
ethnic genocide
state sovereignty
Arab Street
Western imperialism
Mutually Assured Destruction (MAD)
flexible response
calculated ambiguity
nuclear club
Doomsday Clock
jus in bello
"Kill Vehicle"
Minuteman
Strategic Defense Initiative (SDI)
Anti-Ballistic Missile Systems Treaty (ABM)
nuclear blackmail
Brilliant Pebbles
Islamic fundamentalism
primus inter pares

Beginning Legal Research

The goal of POINT/COUNTERPOINT is not only to provide the reader with an introduction to a controversial issue affecting society, but also to encourage the reader to explore the issue more fully. This appendix, then, is meant to serve as a guide to the reader in researching the current state of the law as well as exploring some of the public-policy arguments as to why existing laws should be changed or new laws are needed.

Like many types of research, legal research has become much faster and more accessible with the invention of the Internet. This appendix discusses some of the best starting points, but of course "surfing the Net" will uncover endless additional sources of information—some more reliable than others. Some important sources of law are not yet available on the Internet, but these can generally be found at the larger public and university libraries. Librarians usually are happy to point patrons in the right direction.

The most important source of law in the United States is the Constitution. Originally enacted in 1787, the Constitution outlines the structure of our federal government and sets limits on the types of laws that the federal government and state governments can pass. Through the centuries, a number of amendments have been added to or changed in the Constitution, most notably the first ten amendments, known collectively as the Bill of Rights, which guarantee important civil liberties. Each state also has its own constitution, many of which are similar to the U.S. Constitution. It is important to be familiar with the U.S. Constitution because so many of our laws are affected by its requirements. State constitutions often provide protections of individual rights that are even stronger than those set forth in the U.S. Constitution.

Within the guidelines of the U.S. Constitution, Congress—both the House of Representatives and the Senate—passes bills that are either vetoed or signed into law by the President. After the passage of the law, it becomes part of the United States Code, which is the official compilation of federal laws. The state legislatures use a similar process, in which bills become law when signed by the state's governor. Each state has its own official set of laws, some of which are published by the state and some of which are published by commercial publishers. The U.S. Code and the state codes are an important source of legal research; generally, legislators make efforts to make the language of the law as clear as possible.

However, reading the text of a federal or state law generally provides only part of the picture. In the American system of government, after the

106

legislature passes laws and the executive (U.S. President or state governor) signs them, it is up to the judicial branch of the government, the court system, to interpret the laws and decide whether they violate any provision of the Constitution. At the state level, each state's supreme court has the ultimate authority in determining what a law means and whether or not it violates the state constitution. However, the federal courts—headed by the U.S. Supreme Court—can review state laws and court decisions to determine whether they violate federal laws or the U.S. Constitution. For example, a state court may find that a particular criminal law is valid under the state's constitution, but a federal court may then review the state court's decision and determine that the law is invalid under the U.S. Constitution.

It is important, then, to read court decisions when doing legal research. The Constitution uses language that is intentionally very general—for example, prohibiting "unreasonable searches and seizures" by the police—and court cases often provide more guidance. For example, the U.S. Supreme Court's 2001 decision in *Kyllo* v. *United States* held that scanning the outside of a person's house using a heat sensor to determine whether the person is growing marijuana is unreasonable—*if* it is done without a search warrant secured from a judge. Supreme Court decisions provide the most definitive explanation of the law of the land, and it is therefore important to include these in research. Often, when the Supreme Court has not decided a case on a particular issue, a decision by a federal appeals court or a state supreme court can provide guidance; but just as laws and constitutions can vary from state to state, so can federal courts be split on a particular interpretation of federal law or the U.S. Constitution. For example, federal appeals courts in Louisiana and California may reach opposite conclusions in similar cases.

Lawyers and courts refer to statutes and court decisions through a formal system of citations. Use of these citations reveals which court made the decision (or which legislature passed the statute) and when and enables the reader to locate the statute or court case quickly in a law library. For example, the legendary Supreme Court case *Brown* v. *Board of Education* has the legal citation 347 U.S. 483 (1954). At a law library, this 1954 decision can be found on page 483 of volume 347 of the U.S. Reports, the official collection of the Supreme Court's decisions. Citations can also be helpful in locating court cases on the Internet.

Understanding the current state of the law leads only to a partial understanding of the issues covered by the POINT/COUNTERPOINT series. For a fuller understanding of the issues, it is necessary to look at public-policy arguments that the current state of the law is not adequately addressing the issue. Many groups lobby for new legislation or changes to existing legislation; the National Rifle Association (NRA), for example, lobbies Congress and the state legislatures constantly to make existing gun control laws less restrictive and not to pass additional laws. The NRA and other groups dedicated to various causes might also intervene in pending court cases: a group such as Planned Parenthood might file a brief *amicus curiae* (as "a friend of the court")—called an "amicus brief"—in a lawsuit that could affect abortion rights. Interest groups also use the media to influence public opinion, issuing press releases and frequently appearing in interviews on news programs and talk shows. The books in POINT/COUNTERPOINT list some of the interest groups that are active in the issue at hand, but in each case there are countless other groups working at the local, state, and national levels. It is important to read everything with a critical eye, for sometimes interest groups present information in a way that can be read only to their advantage. The informed reader must always look for bias.

Finding sources of legal information on the Internet is relatively simple thanks to "portal" sites such as FindLaw (*www.findlaw.com*), which provides access to a variety of constitutions, statutes, court opinions, law review articles, news articles, and other resources—including all Supreme Court decisions issued since 1893. Other useful sources of information include the U.S. Government Printing Office (*www.gpo.gov*), which contains a complete copy of the U.S. Code, and the Library of Congress's THOMAS system (*thomas.loc.gov*), which offers access to bills pending before Congress as well as recently passed laws. Of course, the Internet changes every second of every day, so it is best to do some independent searching. Most cases, studies, and opinions that are cited or referred to in public debate can be found online—and *everything* can be found in one library or another.

The Internet can provide a basic understanding of most important legal issues, but not all sources can be found there. To find some documents it is necessary to visit the law library of a university or a public law library; some cities have public law libraries, and many library systems keep legal documents at the main branch. On the following page are some common citation forms.

COMMON CITATION FORMS

Source of Law	Sample Citation	Notes
U.S. Supreme Court	*Employment Division v. Smith*, 485 U.S. 660 (1988)	The U.S. Reports is the official record of Supreme Court decisions. There is also an unofficial Supreme Court ("S.Ct.") reporter.
U.S. Court of Appeals	*United States v. Lambert*, 695 F.2d 536 (11th Cir.1983)	Appellate cases appear in the Federal Reporter, designated by "F." The 11th Circuit has jurisdiction in Alabama, Florida, and Georgia.
U.S. District Court	*Carillon Importers, Ltd. v. Frank Pesce Group, Inc.*, 913 F.Supp. 1559 (S.D.Fla.1996)	Federal trial-level decisions are reported in the Federal Supplement ("F.Supp."). Some states have multiple federal districts; this case originated in the Southern District of Florida.
U.S. Code	Thomas Jefferson Commemoration Commission Act, 36 U.S.C., §149 (2002)	Sometimes the popular names of legislation — names with which the public may be familiar — are included with the U.S. Code citation.
State Supreme Court	*Sterling v. Cupp*, 290 Ore. 611, 614, 625 P.2d 123, 126 (1981)	The Oregon Supreme Court decision is reported in both the state's reporter and the Pacific regional reporter.
State statute	Pennsylvania Abortion Control Act of 1982, 18 Pa. Cons. Stat. 3203-3220 (1990)	States use many different citation formats for their statutes.

114

page:
13: Department of Defense
16: House Armed Services Committee
Press Release, July 18, 2002
22: Associated Press, YONHAP
25: Courtesy CIA
27: Adapted from CNN/USA-Today/
Gallup Poll
34: Associated Press, AP/Thomas Swejck
39: Associated Press, AP
43: Congressional Research Service Issue
Brief for Congress, February 2002

54: Adapted from the National
Resources Defense Council
65: Center for Defense Information
(www.cdi.org)
73: Associated Press, AP/Ron Edmonds
83: "Pushing the Limits: The Decision
on National Missile Defense"—
Coalition to Reduce Nuclear
Dangers and Council for a Livable
World Education Fund. July 2000

ALAN ALLPORT was born in Whiston, England, and grew up in East Yorkshire. He has a Master's Degree in history from the University of Pennsylvania and is currently a Ph.D. candidate at that institution, with a special interest in nineteenth- and twentieth-century European history. He presently is working on projects connected to the social and cultural histories of the British Empire. He lives in Philadelphia.

ALAN MARZILLI, of Durham, North Carolina, is an independent consultant working on several ongoing projects for state and federal government agencies and nonprofit organizations. He has spoken about mental health issues in more than 20 states, the District of Columbia, and Puerto Rico; his work includes training mental health administrators, nonprofit management and staff, and people with mental illness and their family members on a wide variety of topics, including effective advocacy, community-based mental health services, and housing. He has written several handbooks and training curricula that are used nationally. He managed statewide and national mental health advocacy programs and worked for several public interest lobbying organizations in Washington, D.C. while studying law at Georgetown University.